Katrin Hanses

Steel
Construction

Katrin Hanses

Steel
Construction

BIRKHÄUSER
BASEL

Contents

Foreword

Since the start of industrialisation steel has been one of the most important materials in architecture. It allows wide-spanning structures to be built using a minimal amount of material and is therefore highly efficient. There are classic areas where steel is widely used such as shed-type buildings and roof structures, but it also offers an enormous range of possibilities for a wide variety of designs. It makes possible open spaces in which the walls are almost dissolved away; steel can be used to build a wide range of slender spatial structures, creating unusual spatial constellations.

The use of steel (and other metals) is thus closely linked to its technical characteristics and possibilities for construction. Only when armed with knowledge about the particular qualities, the various steel profiles and the principles of fitting together a steel construction, and with an awareness of the material's limitations is the architect in a position to develop creative solutions in steel and constantly to burst through the established limits.

It is at this point that this new book *Basics Steel Construction* begins and gives the reader an understanding of the particular qualities of steel and the possibilities that it offers for different kinds of constructions. By providing knowledge about the building material and its complex constructions and applications it enables architecture students to reflect on creative solutions, including those outside the standardised systems offered by the construction industry. Alongside material research, much of the progress in steel construction has been achieved through innovative and unconventional designs by architects, who have set challenges and provided encouragement for new developments and applications. This book is intended to stimulate its readers, equipped with the knowledge they have gained, to explore the possibilities for their own designs, and perhaps even to develop new approaches to steel construction.

Bert Bielefeld, Editor

Introduction

Ever since humanity has been able to make steel from pig iron, building in steel has grown in importance, in both economic and architectural terms. At the 1889 World's Fair in Paris at the latest the ability to erect pioneering constructions in steel was impressively presented. Before this at the first world's fair, the Great Exhibition of 1851 in London, a number of attempts had been made by Joseph Paxton, among others, to build steel architecture in a way suited to the nature of the material. The construction of the Crystal Palace had already demonstrated the typical of the material. Constructions with large spans could also be easily dismantled. But the destruction of the Crystal Palace by fire in 1936 showed the dangers of this material as well. In planning steel architecture both the positive and negative aspects should be taken into account.

In the meantime, an entire method of building has developed out of the specific qualities of the material, and steel has revolutionised both architecture and civil engineering – for instance, in high-rise buildings and transparent building envelopes, large halls and filigree constructions. In addition, steel is used as reinforcement in concrete, as facade cladding, and in lightweight building. From highly polished scales to a rough surface finish, corroded surfaces and perforations, facade design also has no boundaries for the use of steel.

Its many uses demonstrate just how versatile steel is: from lightweight and small-scale to solid, large cross sections, every kind of structure is imaginable. The dissolution into filigree frame constructions with enormous spans shapes the character of architecture built of steel.

Building material

Steel is a very versatile material that can be used in a wide range of areas. There are very many different kinds of steel and also many standards and regulations for all the parameters of the material, whether in connections, forms or surface treatments. A further factor in the complexity of this field is the very high level of development achieved by production processes and material qualities, which makes this construction material both highly innovative and extremely complex.

MATERIAL PROPERTIES

In contrast to composite materials such as reinforced concrete, steel has a very high compressive and tensile strength, even when not combined with other materials. It is almost equally strong in both these areas. A weakness of the material is its susceptibility to corrosion and thermal deformation, which makes fire protection most important. Consequently, when it is combined with concrete, for instance, special measures must be introduced in order to ensure adequate cover and protection of the steel. Constructional properties

Metals are divided into ferrous and non-ferrous metals. With a carbon content of less than 2%, steel belongs to the ferrous metals. In general, metals have a high density and strength, a high melting point, and good conductivity for heat and electricity.

The many different kinds of steel are classified according to a system of material numbers and letters. > Fig. 1

Position 1 is particularly important for identifying the kind of steel. > Tab. 1 The other positions describe various material properties, the method of production, areas of use, and methods of use, and are of importance primarily for the steel industry. A "G" in front of the letters indicates a cast steel construction part.

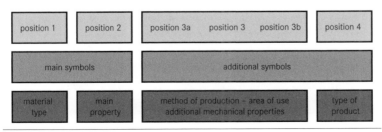

Fig. 1: Concept of the designation system

Tab. 1: Abbreviations for the kinds of steel most often used in building

S	Steels for general steel construction
L	Steels for pipe work construction
B	Steels used on concrete
Y	Prestressing steel

Structural steel

The designation system used for steel was fundamentally altered by the introduction of the European Standards. Two kinds of steel are particularly important for construction: S235 und S355.

What is called fine-grained steel is a particular kind of structural steel. It has high strength and toughness, making it particularly suitable for welded connections. Fine-grained steel achieves these qualities through a reduction of the grain size by using particular elements as alloys, a low carbon content of < 0.20%, and special rolling and heating technology. It has a low weight combined with high strength and is particularly suitable for bridge building. Further grades include high strength and ultra-high strength fine-grained steel, which have even greater elasticity and stress levels.

Weather-resistant structural steel

Weather-resistant structural steel can be used outdoors without corrosion protection. It forms a strong, dense covering layer that protects the building part against corrosion. A development of weather-resistant steel is known as Corten steel, which forms an even patina on the surface and is often used externally as a design element. Building parts made of Corten steel can and should be used in a pre-weathered state so that an even surface can develop. Otherwise, depending on the environmental conditions, irregularities may arise.

Rustproof steel

Rustproof steels are distinguished according to their uses (corrosion-resistant steels, heat-resistant steels), their structure and the essential alloy elements. The short designation begins with an "X".

Corrosion-resistant steels are generally combined under the term "stainless steels". Under normal conditions they form a protective passive coat and therefore generally require no further surface coating. They can easily be used again through melting down; however, a high temperature and much energy are required for production using the arc welding process. > Chapter Building material, Production Stainless steels can be brushed, polished, etched or sandblasted. They can be made as loadbearing building elements, but this requires building approval.

Shaping

When metals are subjected to high stress, plastic deformation takes place (creep). Therefore, in using steel it is not necessarily the failure load that is decisive but the stress at which an expansion of 0.2% is reached. To assess strength, plasticity and elasticity, a stress-strain diagram is usually drawn. > Fig. 2

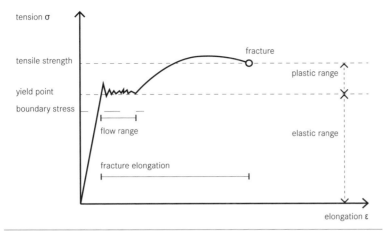

Fig. 2: Typical stress-strain curve of steel

Steel can be used for both the primary and secondary construction. In both cases care should be taken to ensure that there are no gaps in the insulation plane. As steel has high heat conductivity > Tab. 2, there is a particularly great danger of thermal bridges and loss of heating energy at points where the primary construction penetrates, at corners or through gaps in the secondary construction. According to the demands made on the building and building part, individual areas must be thermally separated. > Chapter Building parts, Thermal separation

Insulation

In addition, condensation forms more quickly on the cold surface of the steel than on other materials. Here, ventilation and back ventilation play an important role and can help prevent condensation causing damage to the construction. It must be possible for the water to run off unobstructed and places where condensation could potentially emerge must be identified in advance and avoided. ○

As regards preventing the spread of impact or footfall sound, steel composite slabs behave exactly like a normal reinforced concrete floor slab. Footfall sound must be subdued by a floating screed or resilient

Noise insulation

○ **Note:** For thermal protection of steel frame buildings in summer, the ceiling/floor slabs generally offer the only possibility of accommodating thermal storage mass in the building. Even a 10 cm layer of top concrete at floor slab level produces a noticeable effect. Combination with building part activation is also possible.

Tab. 2: Properties of steel

	Bulk density	Thermal conductivity	Tensile strength	Fracture elongation
Cast steel	$7850\,kg/m^3$	$40-50\,W/mK$	$380-1100\,N/mm^2$	$7-25\%$
Structural steel	$7850\,kg/m^3$	$48-56,985\,W/mK$	$340-680\,N/mm^2$	$17-25\%$
Stainless steel	$7920-7960\,kg/m^3$	$14.5-15\,W/mK$	$500-730\,N/mm^2$	$45-50\%$

constructions. The same applies to airborne noise insulation, which in lightweight steel walls can be improved by low rigidity and flexible facing shells with a high weight per unit area. In general, attention should be given to ensuring complete sound decoupling, above all in building parts such as staircases on which special demands are made in terms of preventing the transmission of impact sound.

PRODUCTION

Iron   Raw materials for the production of steel are coal, coke, iron ore and scrap iron.

○   In the production process iron ores, which are rich in oxides, are mixed with lime and then smelted in blast furnaces to form iron through the introduction of energy (with coke as the source of energy). > Fig. 3 This produces pig iron, which has a high carbon content (3–5%) and contains phosphorus and sulphur. Pig iron is very brittle and not useful as a raw material. The melted pig iron is placed in a converter where oxygen is blown in ("blow") and further materials are added. This reduces the carbon, sulphur and phosphorus content. In producing many kinds of steel, different alloy elements must be added in order to achieve the requisite quality.

The electric arc process > Fig. 4 allows steel to be produced from scrap iron and additives. The arc produces extremely high temperatures so that high-quality alloys can also be smelted and a good steel quality achieved. Steel can be 100% recycled in this way. The process makes extremely sparing use of resources but the high amount of energy required means that it is not particularly economical. Nevertheless, it is used for most steels that must meet high demands in terms of quality.

○ **Note:** Primary production is very energy-intensive. In recent years, however, it has proved possible to increase the efficiency of the production process greatly. Once produced, steel is 100% recyclable and after its initial production has a low demand for raw materials, as scrap iron can be melted down again. However, recycling also has a high energy demand.

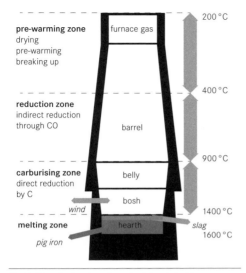

		200 °C
pre-warming zone drying pre-warming breaking up	furnace gas	
		400 °C
reduction zone indirect reduction through CO	barrel	
		900 °C
carburising zone direct reduction by C	belly	
	bosh	
wind		1400 °C
melting zone	hearth	_slag_ 1600 °C
pig iron		

Fig. 3: Sketch showing the principle of the blast furnace

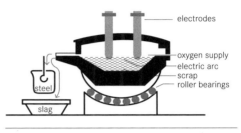

electrodes

oxygen supply
electric arc
scrap
roller bearings

steel

slag

Fig. 4: Sketch showing the principle of the electric arc furnace

Alongside cast iron, steel (structural steel and fine-grained steel) is the most commonly used iron-based material in architecture and civil engineering. Drain pipes, radiators, bath rubs, sewer covers, hydrants, metal fittings and keys are made from various kinds of cast iron. Cast iron is gradually declining in importance and being replaced by better developed material.

Just as there are different ways of manufacturing steel products, there are numerous different methods of processing these products further. A distinction is generally drawn between hot and cold forming. A number of methods can be used in both processes. > Tab. 3 Hot forming generally improves the qualities of the steel and makes it easier to work. Cold forming, in contrast, produces greater strength.

In <u>casting</u>, steel is poured into sand forms. Cast steel parts can be welded but they must first be heated. Cast steel, just like rolled parts, is standardised and designated. Any kind of form is possible, so the scope for design is therefore enormous.

<u>Forging</u> is carried out by hand or machine using hammer and anvil or press moulds. Here, too, a wide variety of different forms can be made. The structure of steel is changed by forging it; the coarse-grained structure is transformed into a fine-grained one, and the strength improved.

<u>Rolling</u> improves the structure of the steel. A system of rollers and drums forms the section under high pressure. This process can be carried out at different temperatures. Rolling is a further development in

Shaping and further processing

Tab. 3: Forming processes

Hot forming	Cold forming
Casting	Drawing
Hot rolling	Cold rolling
Pressing	Pressing
Forging	Forging
	Machining processes
	Folding
	Cold profiling
	Deep drawing

processing the cast steel part. It allows consistent cross sections to be achieved and elongated products with a smooth or textured surface.

Pressing through an opening can also produce the cross section desired. This process is not so suitable for steel and is more useful for non-ferrous metals (e.g. aluminium).

Extruding is generally used for sections that cannot be rolled on account of their geometry. A heated block is pressed through a matrix.

Rods, reinforcement bars and wires are produced by drawing. The material goes through a series of stages in which it is made increasingly thinner. As this is a cold forming process, the products have good strength.

Deep drawing is a method of shaping sheet metal using dies, clamps and matrices. Generally, this process produces sections that are open on one side, troughs or similar products.

There are many other shaping methods, for instance, through mechanical processing. Here, too, there are numerous possibilities. Examples include milling, boring, filing, sawing, turning, bending, stamping and folding. These further processing methods result in what is called a semi-finished product, which then can be worked to form the building part. > Fig. 5

CROSS SECTION PROFILES

Steel products, i.e. the actual building elements and products, are divided into a number of different groups. In the building industry the terms listed below have become established. Given the variety of products, only those main groups of relevance for steel construction are mentioned in order to give a clear overview.

Flat products   Flat products are generally made into semi-finished products, as they have low stability in their original form. Sheet metals are also described as coils but here, too, a distinction is drawn according to thickness

Fig. 5: Semi-finished products

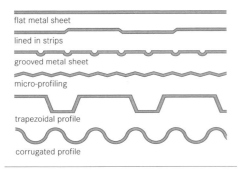

flat metal sheet

lined in strips

grooved metal sheet

micro-profiling

trapezoidal profile

corrugated profile

Fig. 6: Profiled metal sheets

Tab. 4: Sheets and bands according to thickness

Heavy sheet	> 3 mm (e.g. chequered plate)
Thin sheet	< 3.0 mm (e.g. sheet steel)
Ultra-thin sheet	< 0.5 mm (cold rolled)

between hot rolled and cold rolled coils, sheets and bands. > Tab. 4 By folding in trapezoidal and wave forms the necessary stability can be produced along the direction of folding. The building elements remain uniaxially loadable. > Fig. 6 The form is generally given after the coating has been applied. The profiled metal sheets are suitable for multiple layer constructions as both outer and inner shells. At the design stage it should be ensured that the sheets can still be stacked after forming and do result in different transportation sizes.

Flat products are available as corrugated sheets, roof tile shaped sheets, sheets with structured surfaces (chequered, nipple, diamond-patterned or perforated metal) and many others. Profiled metal sheeting is often used to create anti-slip surfaces, and perforated metal sheet is

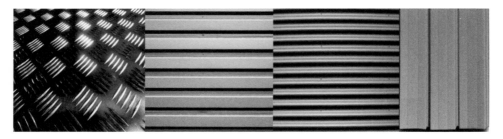

Fig. 7: Flat products

used for facades (e.g. for sun protection). All sheets can be shaped further by folding, and it is possible to combine structured and perforated ● metal sheets. > Fig. 7

A further flat product is expanded metal, which is produced by drawing apart a sheet in which staggered slits have been made. > Fig. 8 This produces a mesh with diamond-shaped openings which, depending on the angle from which the mesh is viewed, make the surface appear to shift between open and opaque. Different degrees of transparency can be achieved using this effect. Expanded metals can also be formed and folded and are often more economical than wire mesh or perforated metal. They also offer a certain degree of stability.

Cables   Cables are used above all in bridge building and high-rise construction. A distinction is drawn between running cables (on rolls, discs, drums) and standing cables (carrier cables, cable slings, guy cables). They consist of cold drawn wire and are generally formed of several wires placed around a core or wire bundle. > Fig. 9

Concrete reinforcement steel   Reinforcement steel is used together with concrete. As concrete handles compressive stress well but tensile stress badly, steel is inserted into it as reinforcement. > Fig. 10 The concrete protects the steel from corrosion by means of sufficient concrete cover. The two materials thus

> ● **Example:** Metal sheeting is often used in industrial building for sandwich panels for roofs and facades. These consist of two profiled steel sheets with insulation between them, and they form an insulated final outer skin that is generally highly economical.

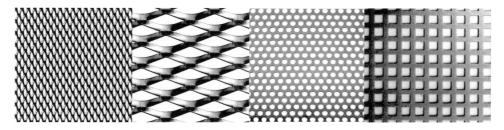

Fig. 8: Expanded metals and perforated metals

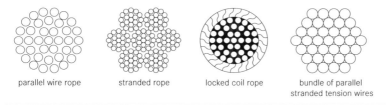

parallel wire rope

stranded rope

locked coil rope

bundle of parallel
stranded tension wires

Fig. 9: Suspension cables (tension cables)

Fig. 10: Reinforcement steel

augment each other extremely well. The reinforcement steel generally provides tension reinforcement in the form of bars, mats or fibres. It is usually warm rolled and has longitudinal and cross ribbing to produce a better bond with the concrete. Prestressed concrete can also be made with steel and is particularly efficient. Short, specially formed steel wire pieces are used as steel fibres and added to fresh concrete. They can replace bar reinforcement and are particularly useful in composite ceiling/floor slabs. > Chapter Building parts, Composite constructions Here, they are used as shear reinforcement and to prevent cracking.

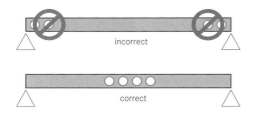

Fig. 11: Correct positioning of holes

Fig. 12: Steel profiles

Profiles   Profiles or sections are known as longitudinal products. They are generally produced by rolling and are available as solid or hollow sections. Solid profiles can be made as round, square, octagonal or flat sections, but for the efficient transfer of forces large and small sections in letter form are normally used. The most commonly found are I, H and U sections (channels) with rounded webs and flanges. I and H sections differ in the width of the flange. > Appendix, Tabs. 8 to 17 Wide-flange beams (HE) are used as columns or beams to handle large loads, whereas normal sections (IP/UP) are generally slender and therefore suitable above all for taking bending stress, for example, as beams. Due to the danger of buckling they are generally not used as columns.

Other sections include angles, T sections, bulb flat sections and various special profiles, for example, for door and window frames. With the standard I or H sections, holes can be made in the web to allow pipes or other services to run through them. These holes should be made only at structurally unimportant places. > Fig. 11

In addition to rolling, profiles can also be produced by extrusion. This process can also be used for thick-walled special profiles. Hollow profiles can also be made in this way. Cold-formed profiles are made by cold rolling metal sheets of low thickness (0.4–8 mm) or by folding. Above all, C and Z profiles are also used as cold-formed profiles. Lips and corrugations ensure better stiffness of the profile. > Fig. 13 Here, too, there are innumerable variations to meet different demands and for different building parts. Cold-formed profiles are particularly suitable as composite building parts.

Hollow sections are drawn seamlessly, rolled or welded (longitudinally or spirally welded) or, occasionally, made from flat products. Hollow profiles are suitable above all for columns and trusses and can have different wall thicknesses. They achieve a high resistance to buckling, but are expensive and sometimes difficult to connect to other building parts, as they do not permit flat surface connections to be made.

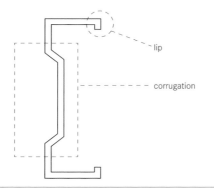

Fig. 13: Lips and corrugations   **Fig. 14: Trapezoidal metal system roof**

Trapezoidal profiles are made from thin metal sheeting using roll pro- Trapezoidal profiles
files. The shaping gives them a degree of stiffness and they can even be
made (uniaxially) loadbearing. > Fig. 14

Some meshes can be made from round or flat rolled wires, rods or Mesh
cables. Different weave patterns can be made and the mesh can be produced in the form of rolls or single areas, or to meet individual demands.
The factors that influence the design include the mesh width, the wire
diameter, mesh thickness and mesh fineness. Flat layers of wire that are
welded or pressed at the junctions are called sheets. Mesh is often used
to make sun protection, for facade elements, in railings and suspended
ceilings, and also as sliding metal curtains.

FIRE PROTECTION

Steel is generally non-flammable; it does not conduct fire and does Building-related
not release any poisonous gases when exposed to fire. However, at high fire protection
temperatures it radically changes its properties. This applies to its tensile
strength, yield point, modulus of elasticity, and the metallic structure.
Planning must respond to these qualities of the construction material. A
number of different areas can be identified regarding fire protection and
prevention. > Tab. 5

Because of steel's tendency to deform radically when subjected to
heat, as mentioned above, particular attention must be given to protect-
ing steel building parts.

This form of fire protection serves to prevent a fire from reaching the
construction in the first place, or delays the heating-up process for so
long that there is a fire-resistance period before failure. The protective
measures should be to restrict the fire, protect from it, or to divert
the heat.

Tab. 5: Types of fire protection

Building-related fire protection	Escape and rescue routes planned, the spread of fire minimised (fire compartments), use of non-flammable/low-flammability construction materials
Technical fire protection	Fire alarm systems, sprinkler systems etc.
Protective fire protection	Direct measures to extinguish and restrict a fire (here building-related fire protection plays a major role)
Organisational and operational fire protection	Preventive measures to avoid fires (e.g. training users for rapid escape and firefighting)

Encasing is one solution. Steel can be encased in sprayed plasters, concrete, or panels and claddings made of mineral fibres. > Fig. 15 The claddings are generally prefabricated box or profile elements that clad the elements flexibly.

Care should be taken that the corrosion protection and encasing harmonise with each other in order to avoid causing damage. Concrete generally combines well with steel and can be used as a fire protection measure with a friction-locked connection. As well as classic concrete with steel reinforcement, spray concrete can be used to provide fire protection to a steel column or columns can encased in concrete.

Coatings that form a fire protection layer include paints and foils, which foam chemically in the event of fire. This kind of fire protection forms a protective layer around the building part and is particularly suitable for steel construction. There is no direct contact with the fire and the building part is screened from the heat for a longer period. This effect only lasts for a certain time and only delays the process of failure.

Protection by means of coatings offers a variety of visual, flexible possibilities. They can be used as part of a colour concept and they also prevent corrosion. A fire protection coating differs from a "normal" coating or varnish only by the roughness of its surface.

Technical fire protection measures consist primarily of fire alarm and sprinkler systems. In addition to the standard measures, water can also be used inside hollow sections to lead away heat. A distinction is made between profiles in which the water stands and those through which water

○ **Note:** A coating of this kind is composed of a corrosion protection primer, the protective coating, and the final coat. Today, a fire resistance rating of F90 and even up to F120 can be achieved using this method.

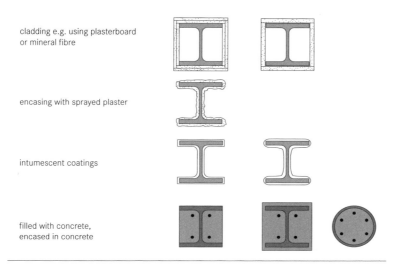

cladding e.g. using plasterboard
or mineral fibre

encasing with sprayed plaster

intumescent coatings

filled with concrete,
encased in concrete

Fig. 15: Fire protection measures

flows. Sections with standing water must be protected by valves against excess internal pressure, and resist heat only for a certain time. Profiles through which water flows can lead the heat away constantly and could, theoretically, be filled with water only if fire breaks out. Generally, however, hydrostatic pressure develops inside a hollow section through which water flows. This should not be underestimated, as it can affect the structural strength of the building part.

In individual cases the elaborate fire protection measures often required in steel construction can be moderated somewhat. On the one hand it is possible to reduce the fire resistance period required. With lower buildings, for instance, we can explain why in the damage resulting from a fire is less serious, or how firefighting measures can be introduced particularly rapidly. On the other hand, active measures such as sprinkler systems or similar can increase the fire-resistance period of the building parts. It is also possible to make a precise structural calculation of the behaviour of the building in the event of fire. What is called a natural fire curve (in contrast to the ISO standard fire curve, which is generally used) can be calculated, which depicts the actual fire load. Then the precise point at which the loadbearing structure will fail in the case of fire can be discovered. A precise analysis of the behaviour of a loadbearing structure during a fire often makes it possible to dispense with a number of extensive fire protection measures.

Proof in the individual case

CORROSION

Iron is a base metal and, as is widely known, its corrosion process involves rust. In the corrosion of metal, a certain amount material is lost, which permanently weakens the structural strength of the building part. The thinner the building part, the more dangerous the rusting process is. As a rule, corrosion starts at a relative humidity of 65% and so building parts made of steel must be given special protection against the corrosion process.

In addition to its effect on function, rust is also undesirable for visual reasons. It suggests a poor quality building part and means the construction is often viewed with distrust.

In buildings it is principally electro-chemical corrosion that is of decisive importance. We distinguish between:

— Surface area corrosion (hollows, hole, gap corrosion)
— Contact corrosion

Corrosion process

Corrosion is an electro-chemical process that takes place in the air, in the ground, or in water. First of all, a compact rust layer builds up, which later becomes loose and flakes off. The loose rust layers also allow condensation to collect at these places, which further encourages the rusting process. Indoors there is no electrolytic moisture film, which is why rust does not occur there. Where, due to corrosion, the surface of the material wears unevenly, we speak of hollow, hole or gap corrosion, ○ depending on the appearance.

By contrast, contact corrosion occurs where different metals touch and where an electrolyte (e.g. water) is occasionally found. Then the more base metal begins to disintegrate. In high-rise buildings this happens above all with facade fixings and roof elements in which different metals meet each other.

○ **Note:** A simplified description of the electro-chemical process: small corrosion elements form on the surface of the steel, each consisting of an anodic and a cathodic area. At the anode an iron ion (FE^{++}) is freed, setting electrons (e^-) free. They naturally wander to the cathode. There on the surface they encounter water (H_2O) and oxygen (O_2), creating hydroxide ions (OH^-). The rust develops at the point where the hydroxide ions meet the iron ion and, in connection with oxygen, oxidise (see Fig. 16).

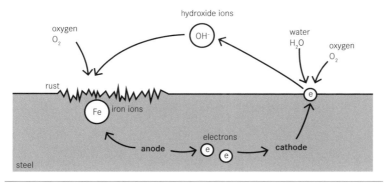

Fig. 16: Schematic depiction of the electro-chemical process

Tab. 6: Corrosion protection

Active	Passive
Design: functional design of the construction and choice of materials	Keeping aggressive materials away from the surface of the building part: artificial covering and protective layers, metallic and non-metallic coverings
Intervention in the corrosion process. Removal/influencing of aggressive materials, intervention in the electro-chemical process	Paints, coatings, coverings, enamelling, galvanising, zinc coating
Reduction of areas for potential attack by corrosion to an absolute minimum	

In processing steel, an electro-chemical reaction can also occur in the building part. This happens, for instance, at welding seams or bent areas, or because of alloy elements. Other materials can accelerate the process. These include, for example, chloride near the sea, or sulphur in industrial regions.

Corrosion can be avoided by proper design. Essentially, the steel construction should be as flat and unarticulated as possible and easily accessible for execution, checking and maintenance to prevent corrosion. Deposits of dirt and water should be avoided. Gaps, slits and joints should be closed, while open voids, hollow boxes and hollow building parts should be given suitable corrosion protection internally and must be ventilated. > Tab. 6

Corrosion protection

SURFACE TREATMENT

There can be a number of different reasons for treating steel surfaces. In addition to design aspects, the need to provide protection against corrosion and fire is decisive here. As regards corrosion protection surfaces, a distinction is drawn between metallic coverings, coatings or a combination of coverings and coating (duplex systems). Surfaces can have very different demands. These can extend from tactile qualities such as roughness, smoothness and hardness to properties that protect the function such as lubricant adhesion or corrosion protection. > Tab. 7 The treatment generally consists of a number of different work processes, often involving both coating and removal operations. In all cases the surface must initially be cleaned and prepared.

Coating   A coating always acts "passively", i.e. it prevents rust and provides a screen against the atmosphere (or the ground or water). The primer coat is the passive coat, while the final coat provides the screen that also protects the primer. Generally the different layers also have different colours so that cover can be ensured. There are also production coatings that provide protection against corrosion during transport, storage and treatment. They do not, however, offer permanent protection.

Before each coating the surface must be properly prepared and freed from any form of dirt, by blasting, pickling, grinding, brushing, and scraping manually or with a machine. The important thing is that the surface should be clean.

No coating is 100% impermeable and it must therefore be applied sufficiently thickly and on a properly prepared base. This can be done by painting with a brush (above all for the primer coat), by rollers or by spraying. The application should be done in dust-free, unchanging conditions, and should be allowed sufficient time to dry.

Coatings are generally based on organic polymers. They can be well adapted to particular situations (corrosion protection) or possibilities of treatment. They are economical to use and offer a wide variety of design options as regards choice of colour and the degree of shininess of the surface. They generally consist of binders, pigments, fillers, solvents or dispersants, and additives. Polymer coatings can become chapped over the course of time and lose their stability.

Metallic coverings   The coatings described above augment the steel surface in an additive way, whereas a metallic covering reacts with the steel surface and becomes one with it. To achieve this, the steel must be covered with a reactive metal (e.g. aluminium or zinc) to allow the electro-chemical binding. The metal most commonly used here is zinc, which absorbs CO_2 from the air, forms a firmly adhering layer, and offers excellent protection against corrosion. As the galvanic layer wears down over the course of time, a sufficiently thick layer should be planned so as to guarantee long-term protection against corrosion.

Steel building parts can be galvanised in a number of different ways. In batch galvanising, the building parts are immersed in a zinc bath and afterwards dried. The size of the pieces must be considered at the planning stage, as there are limitations to the size of the zinc baths. The standard bath size is around $18.0 \times 2.2 \times 3.6$ m (l × w × d); however, long building elements can be immersed from two sides so that they can be twice

Tab. 7: Some examples of surface treatments

Mechanical treatment	Sandblasting	Sand is blasted against the building part using pressurised air.
	Shot blasting	Grainy material with different grain sizes is sprayed against the material using kinetic energy.
	High-pressure water jet treatment	A form of spraying that also removes splinters
	Brushing	Surface cleaning, resulting in a polished surface
	Grinding	Removal of splinters by an abrasive action using grit
	Polishing	No removal of splinters, upstanding material burrs are smoothened, creating a gleaming surface.
Thermal treatment	Flaming	Cleaning of the surface
	Annealing	Cleaning of the surface
Chemical treatment, non-layer forming	Chemical deburring	Fine deburring and smoothening
	Etching	Surface treatment that removes layers; can be used to create visual effects
	Pickling	To remove rust and improve adhesion
	Burnishing	Strongly oxidising solutions create a dense film on the surface.
Chemical treatment, layer-forming	Phosphating	Creates a moisture barrier, a good primer and protection against corrosion, particularly with organic coatings.
	Chromate coating	Formation of chromate layers with aluminium and zinc materials
	Metal spraying	Application of thick metal layers, protects building parts exposed to mechanical stress
	Plating	Covering a steel core with thin, rolled layers of another metal. Composite materials made of different layers result.
	Anodising	Creates an oxidised protective layer on aluminium
	Enamelling	A glass-like non-crystalline enamel is melted onto a steel part and binds with the surface. Acid resistance, corrosion protection, temperature projection and much more
	Chemical and galvanic metalising	More noble metal layers are applied as a surface, e.g. aluminium, chrome, cobalt, nickel, copper, brass, bronze, zinc, silver, cadmium, tin, lead
	Painting	Organic or inorganic polymers combined with binders, pigments, fillers, solvents, additives and water
	Printing	E.g. silk-screening
Metallic coverings	Galvanising	Metallic covering by means of immersion, spraying or similar
	Powder coating	Coloured plastic particles are permanently bound with the steel surface electrostatically.
Coating	Duplex coating	First a metal cover (galvanising), then a coating system
	Plasma-vacuum coating	In a vacuum, chemical elements are applied to the surface (aluminium, copper, titanium etc.). For self-cleansing facade materials, antibacterial surfaces, for colouring stainless steel. Permanent and resistant to deformation.

as long. Coil coating is the term given to galvanising coils and steel strips in a continuous hot-dipping process.

Thermal spraying with zinc (spray galvanising) is used primarily for building parts that cannot be taken apart, or at least not into pieces that would fit into a dip bath. Spray galvanising is relatively expensive but is suitable for improvement purposes. It creates a surface that is irregular and porous, which therefore must always be given a coating.

In electro-galvanising an electric current is introduced into the bath. This exploits the electrostatic attraction of steel and the coating.

Duplex system   If a coating is applied in addition to a metallic covering, the durability of the surface is further improved. This is known as a duplex system. It is often used for visual reasons, to conceal or upgrade the galvanising. A useful side effect is the increased corrosion protection. By combining both methods the building part is protected for a period that is considerably longer than the sum of the protection periods of the two individual measures. A synergetic effect is produced.

Construction methods

Steel as a primary construction offers numerous advantages, such as light and filigree constructions, flexible floor plans and a high degree of prefabrication. However, it also makes demands in terms of fire protection, structural design, and logistics, which must be taken into account from the very start. On a large scale the material can form the loadbearing structure of a building or an engineering structure and is also suitable for filigree individual parts at joints and in secondary structures.

As with every building system, the main function of the loadbearing structure in steel construction is to ensure stability and suitability for the building's function. In this context, stability means transferring all horizontal and vertical forces within the structure as a whole, while suitability for function means that the architecture can used as planned.

LINEAR ELEMENTS

The use of solid web girders is a very common method of linear trans- Girder fer of loads in a building. These are girders with a constant cross section, which in the standard case are subject to bending loads. (See Alfred Meistermann, *Basics Loadbearing Systems,* Birkhäuser Verlag, Basel 2007)

One variation is the girder with a changing height. This means that instead of a constant cross section, the form of the girder is adapted to

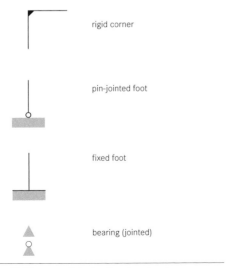

rigid corner

pin-jointed foot

fixed foot

bearing (jointed)

Fig. 17: Elements of the loadbearing structure

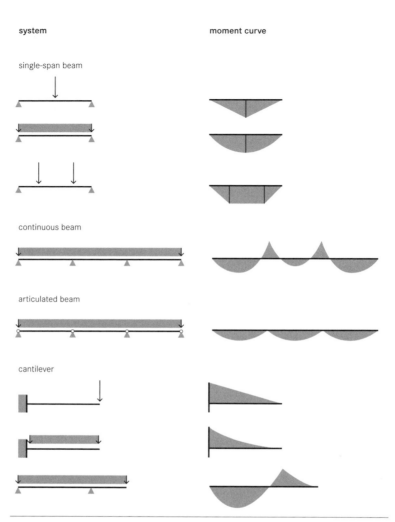

system

single-span beam

continuous beam

articulated beam

cantilever

moment curve

Fig. 18: Moment curves according to system

the moment curve of the building part. > Figs. 18 and 19 This of course has a major impact on the design but can be used to great advantage.

Trussed girders   When solid web girders are not to be used, the solid girder can be broken up to form a truss. This creates a light building element with the appropriate capacity that saves on material. Within the truss the chords take up the moments, while the diagonals and posts transfer the shear forces. > Fig. 20

suitable beam forms

standard parallel chord solid web beam

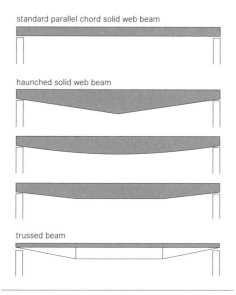

haunched solid web beam

trussed beam

Fig. 19: Single-bay girders, different forms

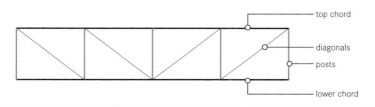

top chord

diagonals

posts

lower chord

Fig. 20: Parts of the truss

A distinction is drawn between braced and post frames. The K truss is a form of post frame. Like the solid web girder, the shape of the truss can be adapted to the moment curve or the form of the roof. The truss can have parallel chords, and sloping or curved upper and lower chords.
> Fig. 22

In designing a truss the designer must consider the structural system. The junctions of the truss are always assumed to be joints at which

Fig. 21: Trusses (from left): fish belly, post truss, angled strut truss

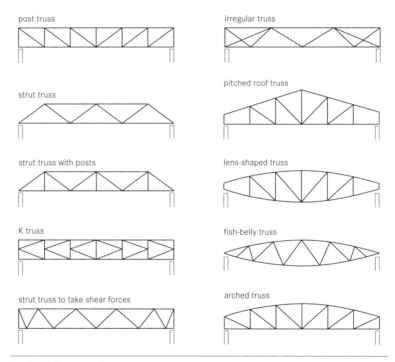

Fig. 22: Various truss forms

the load impacts. Only normal forces occur. Junctions should be centred on the axes of the elements so that the elements of the truss meet at a single point. > Fig. 23 The angles between the elements are between 30° and 60° to the long axis, creating a triangular joint made up of the individual components.

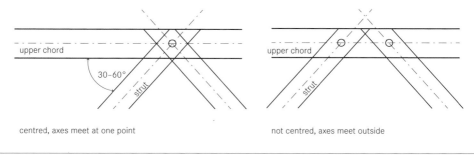

centred, axes meet at one point   not centred, axes meet outside

Fig. 23: Axes in the junctions

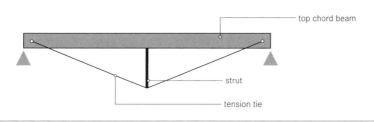

Fig. 24: The parts of a trussed beam

A distinction is made between tension and compression diagonals. Building elements subject to compression forces can be in danger of buckling or tipping over. Here, the length and slenderness of the elements are of particular relevance.

A further variation on breaking up the linear girder is the use of tension ties. This creates single-bay girders with several components. > Fig. 24 The upper chord is the bending beam that takes the bending moment and shear forces, whereas the strut and the tension tie provide support. They are subject only to normal forces and form a hybrid loadbearing structure. ∎

Trussed beams

In contrast to a truss, in which it is assumed that all junctions are pinned, the upper chord in a trussed beam is rigid and continuous. The strut and tension tie are, however, pinned.

> ∎ **Tip:** Evenly trussed beams should be used for symmetrical loads only. They are suitable for roof constructions and also for footbridges or small bridges. They are less suitable for floor loads.

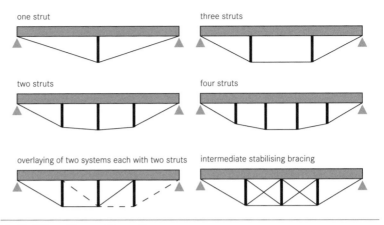

one strut

three struts

two struts

four struts

overlaying of two systems each with two struts

intermediate stabilising bracing

Fig. 25: Different forms of trussed beams

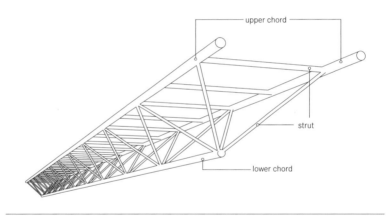

upper chord

strut

lower chord

Fig. 26: Triangular truss

The trussed beam can have several struts and the upper chord can be inclined. > Fig. 25 Up to four struts (arranged symmetrically) make sense. The greater the number of struts, the greater the force on the tension tie, but the moments in the beam are reduced. Several trusses can be combined.

Triangular truss The triangular truss is a special kind of truss. The compression force in the upper chord is taken by two rods creating a three-dimensional truss that performs like a single span. > Fig. 26 Here, too, the upper and lower

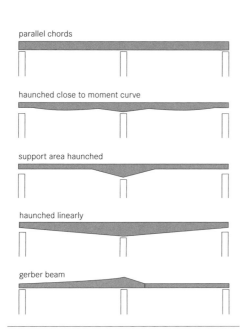

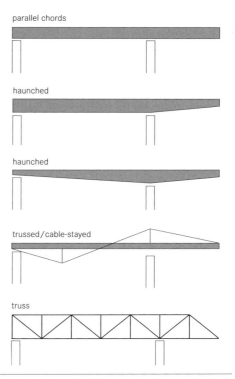

Fig. 27: Examples of continuous beams: approaching the moment curve

Fig. 28: Examples of cantilevers: approaching the moment curve

chord are made as hinged rods, the two rods of the upper chord divide up the forces. Given the number of rods that meet there, the junctions must be designed precisely. > Chapter Building parts, Nodes

    If a beam rests on several bearing points instead of just two, this creates a different structural system. The multi-span beam extends across several spans and a distinction is made between a continuous beam and a Gerber beam. Continuous beams rest without interruption on the various bearing points, producing what is called a structurally indeterminate system (which cannot be determined by the conditions of equilibrium alone). > Fig. 27 Gerber beams have a joint at each bearing point and so produce a series of single-span beams. Multi-span beams can be made as solid web girders, flat and three-dimensional trusses, or as trussed beams.

    If there is no final bearing point at the end of a beam but a projection, the moment curve changes again. A beam with a cantilever can also be adapted to the form of the moment curve. > Fig. 28

Multi-span beams and cantilevers

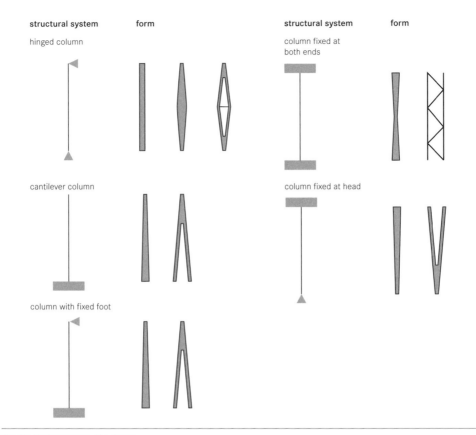

structural system	form	structural system	form

hinged column

column fixed at both ends

cantilever column

column fixed at head

column with fixed foot

Fig. 29: Various types of column

Columns Columns are building elements that are generally subjected to compression forces and are therefore exposed to the danger of buckling. The point of failure and the efficiency of the building part are influenced by its slenderness and the material used for the column. It is not only the size of the cross section that is important but also its geometry. In steel construction, hollow cross sections are particularly suitable for columns.

Columns also differ according to way in which they rest. > Fig. 29 Most commonly used is the pin-ended support, which is hinged at the top and bottom. The end points of the columns, however, can also be fixed or free.

Exactly as with bending beams, it can make sense to adapt the form of a column to the moment curve. A column can also be broken up into several elements.

Frame A frame consists of two or more line-shaped parts that are spanned in a single plane so that they define an area and are connected with each

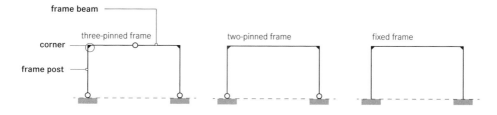

Fig. 30: Principles and elements of a frame

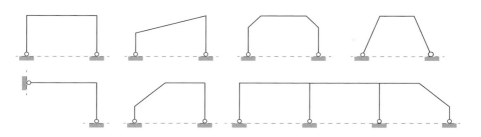

Fig. 31: Selection of different frame systems

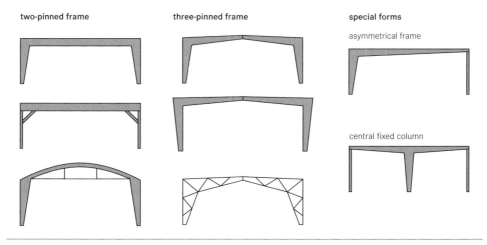

Fig. 32: Selection of different frames

other. There are three-pinned, two-pinned and fixed frames. > Fig. 30 There are numerous design possibilities and frames can also be arranged sequentially. > Fig. 31

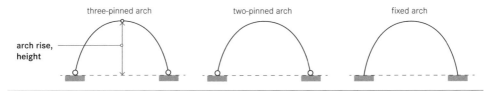

Fig. 33: Principles of the arch

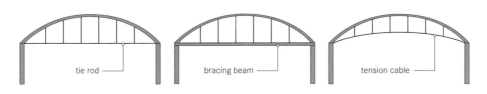

Fig. 34: Possible ways of bracing arches

Essentially, a frame carries and supports and is a system that is rigid in its own plane. It can also function as bracing, both for itself and for a building. The cross sections can be made in different ways. > Fig. 32

Arch   The arch is a form-active structure. This means that its form can be adapted to reflect the flow of forces in the building in such a way that almost no moments occur. It is therefore subject only to normal forces (compression and tension).

To produce exclusively normal forces the individual line of thrust must be calculated. It later provides the structural form. As with frames a distinction can be made between two-pinned, three-pinned and fixed arches. > Fig. 33 In contrast to the cable truss, the arch takes its form from the line of thrust and uses the same principle of a moment-free method of construction.

The lower the height of the arch, the greater the horizontal thrust at the foot, which is of considerable relevance for the structural design. The arch height should therefore be made as great as possible, which in turn has a major impact on the design and on the clear height beneath the arch. An arch can be made as a single structure without columns or it

> ■ **Tip:** In designing the corners of frame, as well as taking structural aspects into account, consideration should also be given to the constraints of the assembly process. A general design rule is that the thicknesses of upright and cross-bar should not differ.

can be raised to allow better use of the space beneath it. Arches can also be broken up into trusses or made more efficient by trussing. There are almost no boundaries set to creativity.

The arch tends to tilt and buckle (see Alfred Meistermann, *Basics Loadbearing Systems,* Birkhäuser Verlag, Basel 2007). Various methods of bracing can be used to counteract the danger of buckling and to achieve greater stability. These can also be integrated into the design of the loadbearing structure. > Fig. 34

SPATIAL ELEMENTS

A planar structure made out of a number of beams is described as a   Beam grillage
beam grillage or beam grid. The loads are transferred in two directions and it is mostly bending load that develops. The beams are rigidly connected to each other, giving a flat, biaxial effect. In design terms the beam grillage is extremely flexible. > Fig. 35 For instance, round plans are also conceivable and a diagonal grid has a favourable impact on the dimensioning of the internal beams.

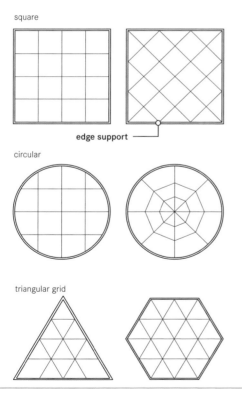

Fig. 35: Beam grillage systems

Fig. 36: Beam grillage on columns, Neue National-galerie, Berlin

Fig. 37: Typical structure of a beam grillage

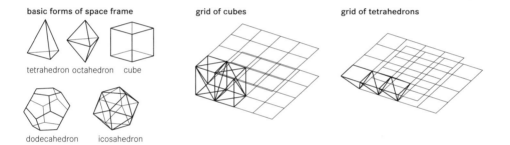

basic forms of space frame

tetrahedron octahedron cube

dodecahedron icosahedron

grid of cubes

grid of tetrahedrons

Fig. 38: Space frame structure

The grillage can bear on pin-joined columns, single columns (fixed) or on wall panels. Just as with the floor plan, the layout of the columns is also flexible. They can be positioned at the outer corners, at internal or edge junctions, with or without cantilevers. > Fig. 37

The loadbearing effect is similar to that of two intersecting beams that transfer the load biaxially. Optimum biaxial load transfer is achieved when the relationship between the sides of the beam grillage is 1:1, as the force always takes the shortest route. In this way the supports are evenly loaded and form an even, rigid system. The edge beams must be made particularly stable, as the internal beams are fixed to them.

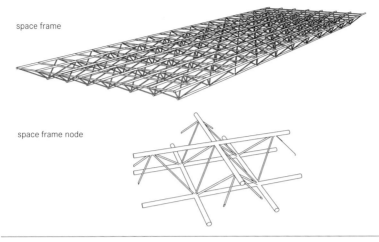

space frame

space frame node

Fig. 39: Space frame

Exactly as with linear systems, in the spatial context, too, the massiveness of the construction can be broken up into a frame. Space frames also consist of rods and junctions with hinged connections to each other. They form a three-dimensional spatial grid consisting of an arrangement of platonic bodies. The forces are transmitted only at the junctions, and the rods are subjected only to compression or tension force.

Forms constructed from triangles are stable without any further measures, whereas forms based on cubes must be combined with additional elements. > Fig. 38 Single-plane space frames are those that together create a flat, planar effect. Structures with low mass and large spans can also be created in a single plane.

Thanks to its stability the planar space frame works like a plate or a beam grillage so that no additional horizontal bracing is necessary. It has a highly filigree quality, and is light and very efficient.

Space frames are generally built using circular sections, although square section tubes are sometimes used. > Fig. 39 Junctions can be made by welding, using spheres, or slit metal sheets. > Chapter Building parts, Nodes

Shells and domed structures can be constructed from space frames that are not planar. One example is the geodesic dome, which is composed of dodecahedrons or icosahedrons.

Fig. 40: Cable structure for bridge building, Brooklyn Bridge, New York

SPECIAL FORMS

Suspension constructions

In suspension constructions, external loads are directed through structural elements subjected to tensile force. The design possibilities of suspended constructions are very varied, particularly with large spans. > Fig. 40 The low dead weight and the almost exclusively tension load ensures optimal exploitation of the material. The stability is not endangered by excessive compressive loads.

In contrast to the arch, which exploits the ideal thrust line of a building part, in suspended constructions the optimal cable line can be used as an approach. It describes the ideal for a structure in which no moments are released and which can therefore be made in a very filigree way. Cable structures are minimal structures and are therefore often used for especially large constructions, such as bridges or big halls. A cable is unable to take bending moments and its form always follows the applied loads. This results in a precise approach to the cable line.

However, calculating suspension structures is a complex process, and complicated joints and anchorage points can be involved. The tension forces that are favourable for slender steel elements are very unfavourable for the foundations, which in principle transfer loads to the ground by means of compression. Elaborate anchoring in the ground is required at times. In building suspension structures it must be ensured that the cables never lose tension or droop, as this could result in loss of stability.

Ensuring stability is, in general, one of the major challenges of a suspension structure. In a suspended roof, for example, stabilising can be done by means of weight or by using a roof skin with a stiffening shell effect. > Fig. 41

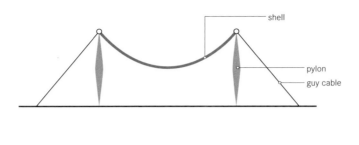

Fig. 41: Stabilising suspension constructions

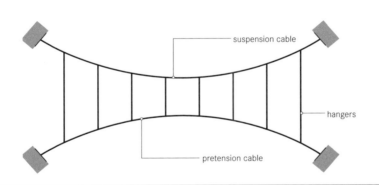

Fig. 42: Cable truss

Cable trusses achieve their stability through uniaxially arranged, pre- Cable trusses
stressed, counter-curved cables. Cable trusses consist of a loadbearing
cable and a tension cable, which are normally connected to each by tension elements known as hangers. > Fig. 42 If these are omitted, then as with
trussed beams, struts must be used. > Fig. 43 These trusses are primarily
endangered by buckling of the struts or twisting of the truss.

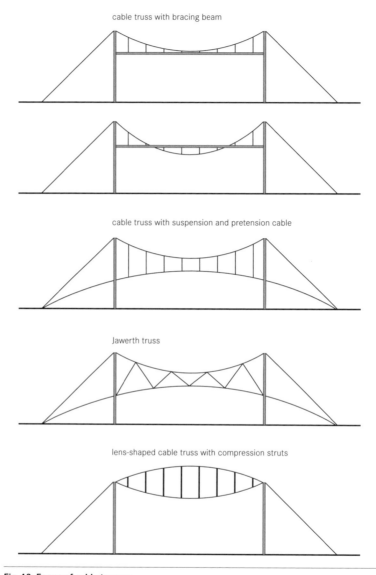

cable truss with bracing beam

cable truss with suspension and pretension cable

Jawerth truss

lens-shaped cable truss with compression struts

Fig. 43: Forms of cable trusses

A variation on the cable truss is the cable-stayed truss. Whereas cable trusses are very delicate but difficult to manufacture, the cable-stayed truss offers greater potential. It contributes to greatly simplifying production, above all in the case of bridges. Within the construction, a

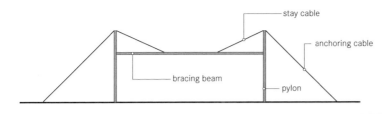

Fig. 44: The elements of a cable-stayed truss

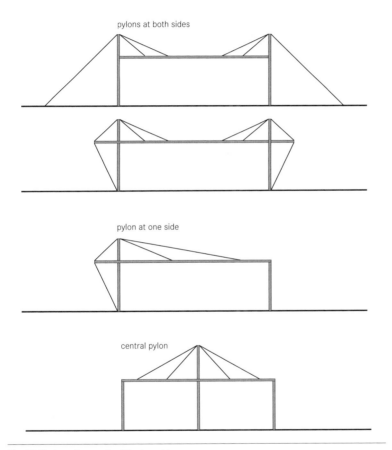

Fig. 45: Various forms of cable-stayed trusses

slender girder is suspended from cables and works as a stiffening girder.
> Fig. 44 It is subject to normal forces. The cable-stayed truss allows a wide variety of solutions in the design and arrangement of the cables and pylons. > Fig. 45

Fig. 46: Cable-stayed trusses in the National Stadium in Warsaw with a suspension bridge in the foreground

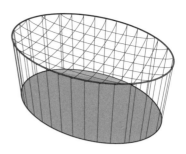

Fig. 47: Closed cable net

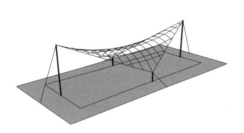

Fig. 48: Open cable net

Fig. 49: Open cable nets: Olympiapark and Stadium, Munich

Cable net   Cable nets function primarily as a membrane. Cable nets are made of multitudes of anticlastic, stressed loadbearing and tension cables and in this way acquire stability. A distinction is drawn between open and closed cable nets. > Figs. 47, 48 and 49 In the closed cable net the cable tension forces are directed into edge bearings. These are subject to compression and the edge beams allow a usable space to be formed.

Cable nets can, for instance, form the substructure for a light roof skin. The more densely the cables are woven together, the more the construction functions as a membrane. The elements, which are subjected only to tension forces, can be rods or cables made of steel.

Planning principles

In steel construction the loadbearing structure is always a part of the design. From the very start it is important to match design concepts with constructional possibilities. The structure can be used as a design element and made entirely visible, or it can be concealed between the layers of the construction. > Fig. 50 The relationship of the building shell and spatial enclosure to the structure should also form a part of the basic concept of the building.

Having examined the individual elements of the structure, an approach will now be made to implementing the principles learned. Particular attention is given to the influence on the architectural planning.

HALL CONSTRUCTION

In general we can differentiate between single-storey and multi-storey steel buildings. The possibilities steel offers for large, column-free constructions that are light but efficient make it predestined for industrial and shed or hall building. > Fig. 51 The loadbearing elements discussed earlier are often employed precisely in this field.

Generally, large spans are handled by column-beam systems. Depending on the kind of bracing used, these are combined to form a frame or spatial constructions. The building's function may mean the bracing in hall building has to handle wind loads as well as the impact loads of vehicles or the loads of indoor cranes.

Primary construction

With low distances apart of approx. 6–7 m, roof and facade constructions can rest directly on the column-beam systems. > Chapter Planning principles, Lightweight construction

■

If the construction axes in the primary construction are larger, a secondary structure may be required as bearing for the building envelope. The main beams, which can also be called girders, can be solid web girders or trusses. They can also be optimised by adapting them to the moment curve. In smaller building volumes, elements with parallel chords are often used for economic reasons.

Secondary construction

> ■ **Tip:** Here, special structural calculations must prove the ability of roof and facade constructions to handle shear forces and they must be constructed in a special way (e.g. bolted). Many manufacturers offer ready-made tested systems to meet different demands (spans, profile thickness etc.).

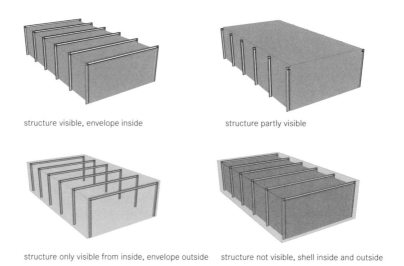

structure visible, envelope inside

structure partly visible

structure only visible from inside, envelope outside

structure not visible, shell inside and outside

Fig. 50: Position of the loadbearing structure

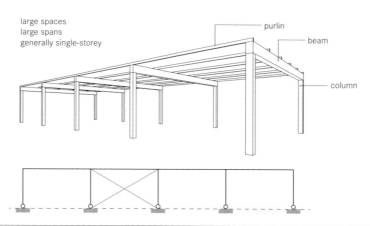

large spaces
large spans
generally single-storey

purlin

beam

column

Fig. 51: Principle of hall building

Fig. 52: Hall building with primary construction of solid web beams and secondary struts

In constructing the secondary structure for roofs, use is often made of purlins, which are placed at right angles to the loadbearing system and provide a flat substructure for the roof skin or construction layers. > Chapter Building parts, Roof

The same applies to the construction of the walls where posts can form the secondary construction. As they are less affected by the transfer of loads and weathering they are on a smaller scale. The secondary construction also requires a bracing cladding in order to prevent tilting or deformation. > Fig. 52 Consequently, the primary and secondary construction and the external envelope must be designed together as parts of an overall system.

MULTI-STOREY CONSTRUCTION

In contrast to a single-storey hall building, a multi-storey building connects several structural systems that rest upon each other in sequence. > Fig. 53 This produces different requirements for structure, fire protection, sound insulation and, naturally, also the design. Bracing has also to be planned. Stacked frame systems are often used with vertical trusses as bracing.

Multi-storey buildings up to the height of high-rise structures with steel constructions are generally built as skeleton frames, which are characterised by the flexibility of the floor plans they allow and which reduce loadbearing building parts to a minimum. The steel constructions, > Chapter Construction methods which are very close to optimal load transfer within the building parts, make good sense here. The system is made up of a combination of panels (slabs), columns and the appropriate bracing elements. > Chapter Planning principles, Bracing The structural elements include beams,

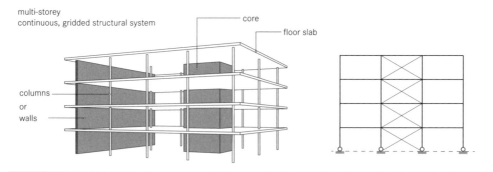

multi-storey
continuous, gridded structural system

core

floor slab

columns
or
walls

Fig. 53: Principle of multi-storey building

columns, frames, panels, or panels broken up into cross-bracing. Solid panels are generally made up of composite elements > Chapter Building parts, Composite constructions and can also incorporate additional building services functions.

LIGHTWEIGHT CONSTRUCTION

Lightweight construction comprises light, thin-walled building parts of steel; the aim is to combine the minimised use of material with other positive effects. Lightweight building allows speedy progress of construction work and a high level of prefabrication. It also simplifies the integration of services and produces high-quality building work.

Frame systems   Lightweight construction is often used in individual building parts such as facade or roof constructions, but is also suitable for the erection of entire buildings. Here, frame systems are generally used. > Fig. 54 Similarly to timber building, the "platform frame" or the "balloon frame" system can used. These systems differ in terms of construction and assembly. Lightweight construction also allows larger building elements to be prefabricated and simply mounted in place on site. For example, entire hotel bedrooms complete with the interior fittings can be delivered to the building site.

○ **Note:** The platform frame method describes a system that allows a high degree of prefabrication and element manufacture. The wall elements stand on the floors, allowing storey-wise construction. The balloon frame system has continuous, multi-storey posts and the floor slabs run beside or in front of the posts or columns (see Figs. 58 and 59).

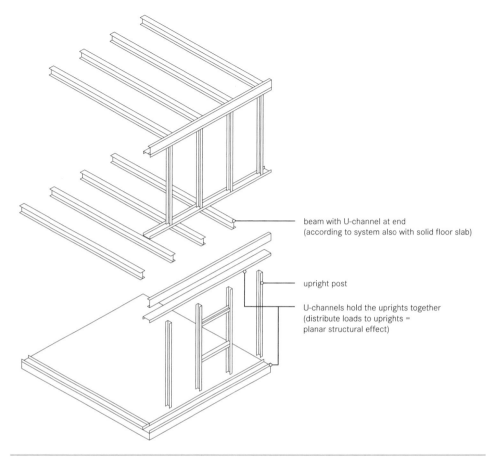

beam with U-channel at end
(according to system also with solid floor slab)

upright post

U-channels hold the uprights together
(distribute loads to uprights =
planar structural effect)

Fig. 54: Principle of frame construction

The bracing of lightweight construction buildings must be carefully considered. Wind loads cannot always be taken by the floor slabs, and essentially bracing should be provided in at least two directions. The bracing generally takes the form of cross-struts in the walls in at least two directions. In some cases measures must be taken in lightweight constructions to prevent lifting due to wind suction.

Light facade systems are used primarily in industrial building. Sandwich elements are economical and offer a variety of design options for the surface finish through profiling and the use of colour. They consist of an external and an internal steel sheet that can be filled with various insulation materials. > Fig. 57 While they are suitable for wall and floor slab constructions, they generally require a secondary construction (purlins or similar) as support.

Facade lightweight systems

49

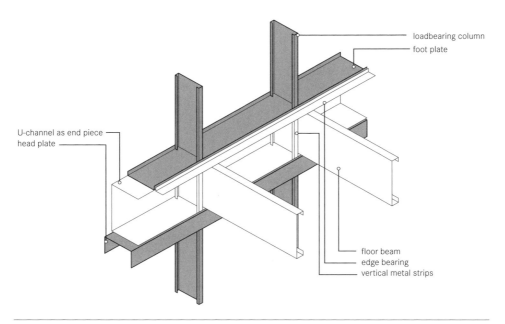

loadbearing column

foot plate

U-channel as end piece
head plate

floor beam
edge bearing
vertical metal strips

Fig. 55: Principle of the platform frame construction method

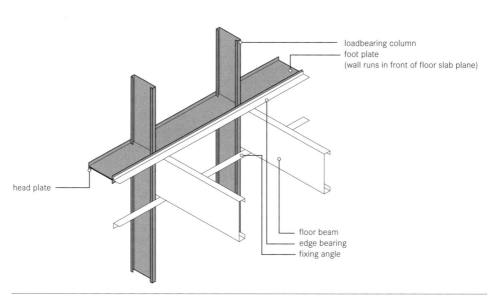

loadbearing column
foot plate
(wall runs in front of floor slab plane)

head plate

floor beam
edge bearing
fixing angle

Fig. 56: Principle of the balloon frame construction method

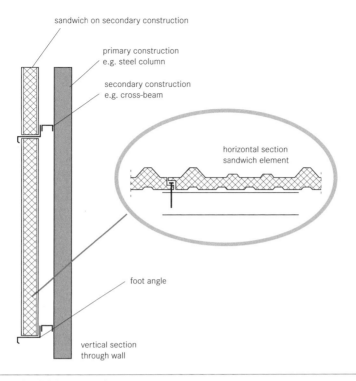

sandwich on secondary construction

primary construction
e.g. steel column

secondary construction
e.g. cross-beam

horizontal section
sandwich element

foot angle

vertical section
through wall

Fig. 57: Sandwich construction system

Two layer systems with independent shells can be used more flexibly. Trapezoidal metal sheeting is often used for individually designed roof constructions and can have a uniaxially bracing effect. > Fig. 58 There are numerous possibilities for roof and wall constructions, with or without back ventilation.

Profiled liner trays can form the wall, the bracing and the construction. The elements are built up like a sandwich element and can meet different demands for the surface. They can be so stably connected to each other that they form a construction joint. Here, they are stacked vertically on top of each other and can additionally be filled with insulation and, for instance, closed with a vertically positioned trapezoidal sheet. > Fig. 59 The sandwich element made in this way can be used both vertically and horizontally.

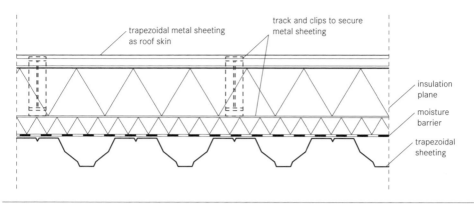

Fig. 58: Example of a roof construction with trapezoidal sheeting

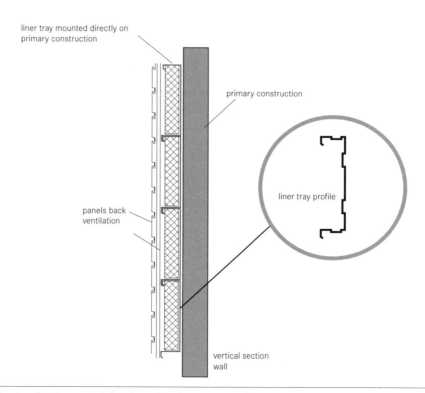

Fig. 59: Liner tray facade mounted directly on the primary construction

Many kinds of metals can be used for facades. Alongside steel, stainless steel and weather-resistant structural steel, aluminium, copper and zinc facades (non-ferrous metals) are common. Metal facades are durable, require little maintenance and are often very light due to their low material thickness.

As metal is almost completely impervious to moisture, care must be taken to ensure that no condensation forms. Air supply and extract openings in the facade must be planned. In addition, a moisture barrier may be required on the inner face.

In designing metal facades, particular attention must be paid to the thermal deformation of the material. Expansions up to a length of 1.2 mm/m can easily occur. To avoid damage due to deformation or constraints the facade should be able to move and must be fixed flexibly to the substructure.

Wind suction forces on the facade may also affect the fixings. The corrosion protection must be considered when choosing the surface and placing the building elements and upstands. Water should not be able to collect or to enter joints.

BRACING

Every building volume and every section of a building volume must be braced in itself. The bracing serves to take horizontal forces such as wind loads or earthquake movements. The building volume must be protected against twisting and displacement, using bracing in both horizontal and vertical directions.

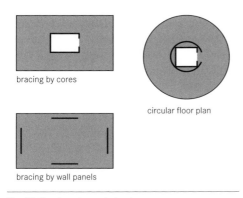

bracing by cores

circular floor plan

bracing by wall panels

Fig. 60: Bracing elements in plan

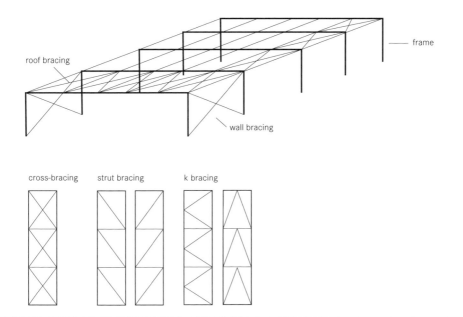

roof bracing

frame

wall bracing

cross-bracing   strut bracing   k bracing

Fig. 61: Various kinds of bracing

Bracing by cores   Horizontal loads can be transferred, for example, by stiff building parts, such as circulation cores or sanitation facilities, which are made of a solid material (concrete) and positioned within the skeleton frame construction. > Fig. 60 Horizontal forces are conducted from the facade through the floor slab plates to the bracing core. Lightweight floor slab constructions of steel, which do not have a plate effect through being combined with concrete or similar, must be formed as a plate by means of cross-bracing. The vertical bracing cores, walls, frames and fixed columns then direct the loads into the foundations. A system made up of horizontal and vertical bracing elements develops.

Bracing by struts   In hall or frame constructions the bracing is provided by strutting, also in both vertical and horizontal planes. > Fig. 61 The bracing must be arranged in longitudinal and transverse directions and in both wind directions. Frames can also be used to provide bracing in the transverse direction.

There should be at least three bracing elements: their lines of action should not meet at a point and they should not all run parallel. In multistorey buildings, bracing elements must be placed on each floor level. They should stand axially above each other so that they can transfer the loads directly.

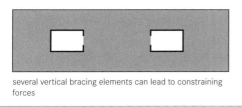

several vertical bracing elements can lead to constraining forces

Fig. 62: Possible constraining forces due to two cores

Fig. 63: Profile is raised into position

Particular attention must be paid to preventing constraining forces developing between two or more bracing elements. For example, having two circulation cores within a rigid floor slab leads to an increased risk. > Fig. 62

Avoiding constraining forces

TRANSPORT SIZES AND ASSEMBLY

In assembling steel buildings, elements up to a particular size are prefabricated in the factory, given corrosion protection or a coating, and then transported to the construction site. The building parts are then lifted into position using a crane and bolted together so that, for example, the structural design of the bracing must also take into account temporary situations during assembly. With larger building parts, building stages must be planned for steel construction, too. Both production and transport sizes are subject to certain restrictions (e.g. bridges under which the transport vehicles must pass) and these must be considered at the planning stage. If the measures required for a building part exceed one of these parameters, then construction joints must be made on the building site. > Chapter Building parts, Assembly or site joints

Steel construction is generally very precise, which often leads to difficulties when combining steel with other materials that have larger dimensional tolerances. Adapting steel construction on the building site

Dimensional tolerances

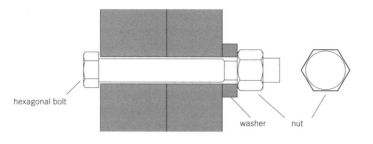

Fig. 64: Principle of a bolt connection

is either not possible at all or possible only to a very limited extent. Bolted connections allow somewhat more flexibility, through the use of oversized or slotted holes and the possibilities offered by assembly on the building site. In contrast, welded connections are practically unchangeable and making them on the building site is extremely difficult; therefore, where possible, welding work should be carried out only in the factory.

Consequently, all details and connections must be planned precisely and must be able to handle dimensional tolerances. Assembly joints are also an integral part of the planning. Architecture and structural design should therefore correspond closely with each other.

CONNECTIONS

The design and execution of connections is a particular challenge in steel construction. The function of connections in general is to transfer forces from one building part to another (tension, compression, bending, torsion) and to meet particular aesthetic and building law requirements (e.g. on fire protection or building physics). A distinction is made between detachable and non-detachable connections.

Detachable connections

Detachable connections include screw, pin and bolt connections. > Fig. 64 The regulations commonly referred to provide guidelines for the distances to edges and between holes and the arrangement of the screws or bolts. For a lighter assembly, for example, at least two bolts per connection should be assumed.

Pin and bolt connections are suitable for connections in which shear forces arise. In pin connections, pins or studs that fit precisely are placed in steel or cast steel pieces. This connection is positive and non-positive. Here, too, the forms and dimensions are governed by standards. Two or more building parts can be connected with each other.

The difference between pin and bolt connections is that in the bolt connection at least one part remains movable. > Figs. 65 and 66 A further distinction is made between bolts with and without a head. In pin or stud

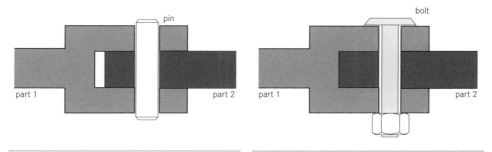

Fig. 65: Principle of a pin connection   **Fig. 66: Principle of a bolted connection (without nut)**

connections, all parts are fixed rigidly together. The most commonly used pins are cylinder pins, taper pins, spring pins, and dowel or groove pins.

Non-detachable connections include welding, riveting and soldering, and to a limited extent also adhesive connections. Welded connections are best made in the factory, as conditions on the construction site are not always suitable for this kind of work. They are used, for example, when several individual cross sections are to be fixed together to form a single cross section. In fitting individual building parts together, welded connections do not allow the same level of precision as bolted connections.

So that they fulfil the structural function of transferring forces at a connection, weld seams must be made according to particular requirements. Among the various kinds of welds, butt welds and fillet welds are perhaps the most common. > Fig. 67 A butt weld connects pieces that butt up against each other on the same plane. The edges that will form the connection must be prepared first, by grinding, milling, or flame cutting. A fillet weld is required where two building parts meet at an angle or at right angles. Fillet welds can also be made from two sides. A distinction is drawn between coved welds, flush welds and camber welds.

Particularly thick welds must be made in several layers. First come what are called the root layers, then the filling, and finally the covering layer. When two materials of different thicknesses meet, the lesser thickness determines the thickness of the welding seam. There are various forms of seams. I, V, HV, DV and Y seams are particularly often used.   ○

Non-detachable connections

○ **Note:** Welded connections may be made only by certified skilled workers. There are various welding certificates that prove this competence. Companies holding a major welding certificate can produce all constructions in steel building without restrictions. Those with a minor certificate are subject to certain restrictions.

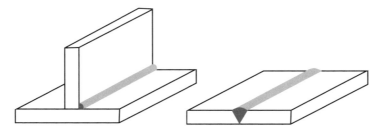

Fig. 67: Butt and fillet welds

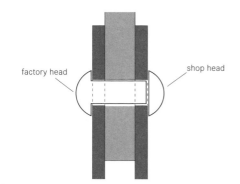

factory head   shop head

Fig. 68: Riveted connection

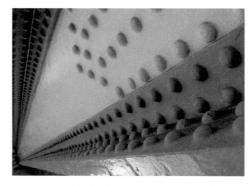

Fig. 69: Rivets

Rivet connections are rarely used today. They demand a considerable amount of work and are therefore uneconomical. They are used for positive or non-positive connections and are subjected to shear force. They should not be subjected to axial tension. In addition, they should consist of the same material as the building parts they connect. > Figs. 68 and 69

As with welding, soldering also creates a firmly bonded connection between two building parts. The connection is rigid and tight. However, a soldered connection is made at lower temperatures. Depending on the soldering process used, the connection can later be released by applying heat to it, whereas with welding the surface of the building parts is permanently changed and they can be released only by destroying the connection.

The advantage of this kind of connection is that the building parts are not weakened by penetrations. However, larger areas of soldering are uneconomical and they require even more intensive preparation work than welded connections.

The principle of glued connections is relatively young and is, in part, still at the development stage. The low temperature stability in the case of a fire represents a problem. Adhesive connections are suitable for composite building materials or sandwich elements.

Building parts

CORNERS

Frame corners are characterised by their bending stiffness. The decisive aspect is that the parts that meet should not be able to twist apart under loading. To produce this stiff effect the frame corners must be made in a particular way, generally by means of special stiffening measures. > Fig. 71 Frame corners can be welded or put together using pre-stressed high strength bolts. > Fig. 70 The angle at the frame corner does not have to be 90° but can be adapted to suit the roof form, for instance, for inclined roofs.

FEET

A foot must always be planned in detail when a vertical, pointed build-ing part is to transfer the forces to a horizontal building part, generally the foundation. Making this point properly is extremely important for the correct transfer of forces. Such vertical building parts include columns and frame posts.

Simple foot

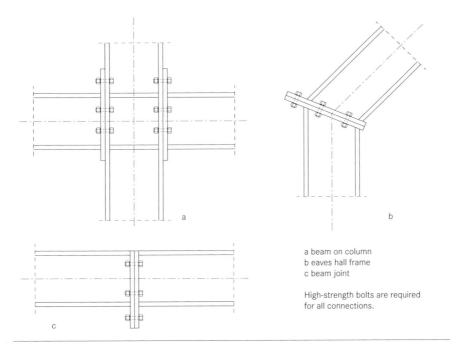

a beam on column
b eaves hall frame
c beam joint

High-strength bolts are required for all connections.

Fig. 70: Examples of frame corners with head plates, bolted

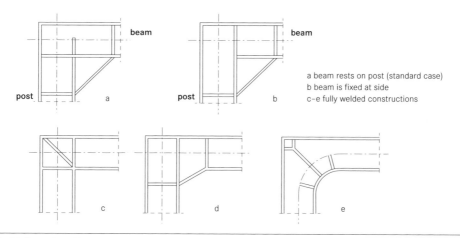

a beam rests on post (standard case)
b beam is fixed at side
c–e fully welded constructions

Fig. 71: Examples of frame corners with stiffening

Feet are generally either pinned (hinged) or fixed. However, there is a special case when, in structural design terms, the column is planned with a pinned foot but in reality only tranfers a central compressive load to fixed structures. In multi-storey buildings this is the case with columns, for example. The feet are then made with footings and are not pinned. Instead, load-distributing footings are made and filled with expanding mortar. A joint of between 2 and 4 cm should be made between the concrete building part and the steel head plate. The mortar ensures the even transfer of the load to the ground and also compensates for unevenness and dimensional tolerances in the footing or base plate. To prevent twisting occurring later at the bearing point, the mortar joint must be produced precisely and evenly. > Figs. 72 and 73 With greater loads or in ground with poorer bearing capacity, the foot plate is stiffened. > Fig. 74 The introduction of stiffening plates, however, leads to shear loads in the steel building element and they must be especially calculated according to the cross section of the profile. If shear force also occurs at the foot it is best transferred to the foundation by means of shear cleats. Special measures must also be introduced if moments or tension forces occur.

Fixed foot   If the structural situation means a post or column needs to be fixed rigidly, the foot must be constructed to meet this requirement. This is necessary, for example, in the case of cantilever columns or frame posts with fixed feet. The greater the forces occurring at the foot, the greater the stability of the construction must be. Where high fixed-end moments occur, foot cross-bars are used. > Fig. 75 They ensure that the moment from the column is transferred to the foundation. Fixed foot constructions can also be made with prestressing.

Fig. 72: Foot of a steel column

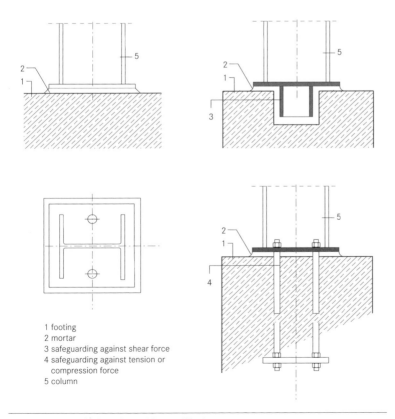

1 footing
2 mortar
3 safeguarding against shear force
4 safeguarding against tension or
   compression force
5 column

Fig. 73: Example of a foot plate without stiffening

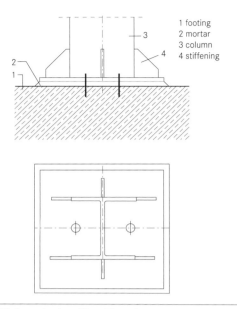

1 footing
2 mortar
3 column
4 stiffening

Fig. 74: Example of a stiffened foot plate

A further way of making a fixed foot is the sleeve foundation. Here, the steel column or post is placed in a prefabricated concrete sleeve into which concrete is then poured. > Fig. 76 This construction ensures a high level of fixing but is not always advisable. The transition from the concrete to the exposed steel part is later subject to corrosion. In addition, the concrete filling makes this kind of fixing more suitable for I profiles than for hollow profiles. Dismantling is possible only by cutting through the column.

Pin-ended or hinged foot   With a pin-ended column in slidable structures or frame posts with a hinged joint, the foot is also made as a joint. Here, constructions with a ball-like centring piece or cleat are generally used. Connections with real bolts are made only for light constructions and are rare. > Fig. 77

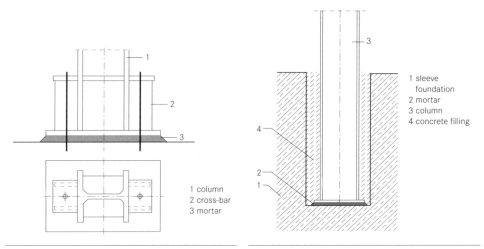

1 column
2 cross-bar
3 mortar

1 sleeve
foundation
2 mortar
3 column
4 concrete filling

Fig. 75: Example of a fixed foot with foot cross-bar   **Fig. 76: Example of a sleeve foundation**

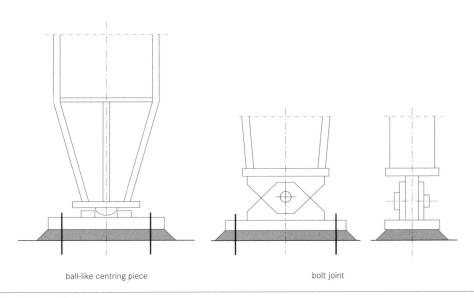

ball-like centring piece   bolt joint

Fig. 77: Hinged foot

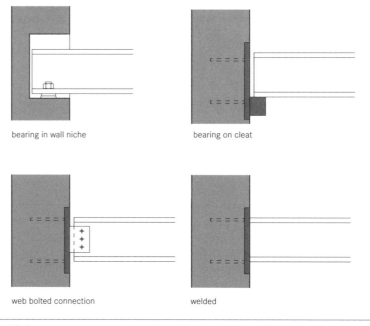

bearing in wall niche

bearing on cleat

web bolted connection

welded

Fig. 78: Beams on masonry or concrete

SUPPORT

Beam resting on wall

When a steal beam rests on a wall construction the connection to materials with high tolerances represents a special challenge. > Fig. 78 The support or bearing point must be made in such a way that it can transfer all the loads across its entire area. A layer of mortar beneath the beam ensures a non-positive locking connection.

Beam resting on beam

When beams meet each other at right angles in different planes their webs can be cut away at the junction and given appropriate strengthening. > Fig. 79

In exceptional cases, beams that intersect at the same height can pass through each other. Generally, however, a joint is formed, usually with bolted connections employing double angles or head plates. > Fig. 80

Beam resting on column

The simplest form of jointed connection between a beam and a column uses a head plate. This can be constructed as a non-sliding system or as a continuous beam. > Fig. 81

For instance, if angular rotation of the beam is to be expected, this leads to off-centre loading of the column. Additional measures must then be employed in making the bearing, for instance, a centring element.

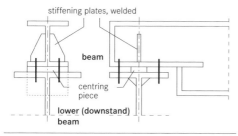

Fig. 79: Examples of notched, intersecting beams

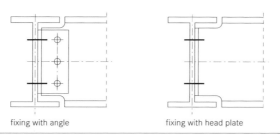

fixing with angle

fixing with head plate

Fig. 80: Example of bolted connections with double angle and head plate

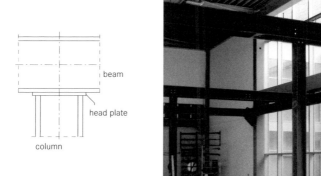

Fig. 81: Head plate as bearing

Fig. 82: Bearing point at continuous column (reinforced concrete)

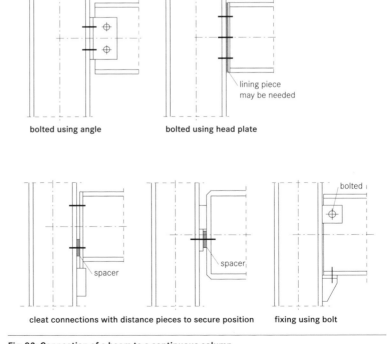

bolted using angle

bolted using head plate

lining piece
may be needed

cleat connections with distance pieces to secure position

spacer

spacer

fixing using bolt

bolted

Fig. 83: Connection of a beam to a continuous column

There are several ways of connecting a beam to a continuous column Connecting beam to column or post. Here, too, angles or head plates are generally used. One variation is a connection using cleats. > Figs. 82 and 83

ASSEMBLY OR SITE JOINTS

The compression forces within a multi-storey building increase con- Column joints tinuously from top to bottom. The dimensions of the column cross section can, theoretically, be adapted to this situation. At the joints, connections must be made that can balance the difference in size. Where cross sections are almost identical, butt welds can be made relatively easily. Hollow sections, in contrast, generally require a flat steel to provide the necessary bearing area. This is particularly important with joints that are made on the building site. Maintaining the axes of the two joints represents a challenge: auxiliary constructions generally need to be employed.

Assembly joints (i.e. assembly on site) are occasionally made using flange and web straps. Where cross sections are different, filler plates must be used, as with beam joints. Joints are often made using head plates. Where different profiles meet a gradual, continuous transition (a) can be made or an intermediate element (b) can be used; where the angle is steeper, transverse stiffening plates are needed (c). > Fig. 84

Another variation is the use of intermediate plates that take up the difference in cross section. In the case of bolted joints a head plate is fixed to each column part. > Fig. 85

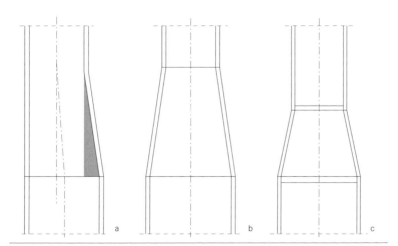

Fig. 84: Joints between cross sections of different sizes

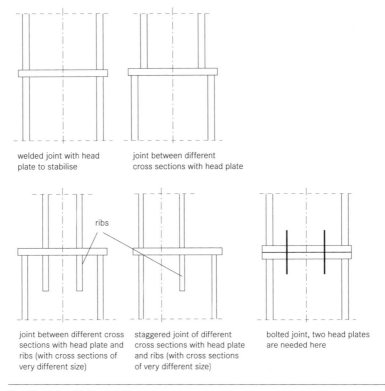

welded joint with head
plate to stabilise

joint between different
cross sections with head plate

ribs

joint between different cross
sections with head plate and
ribs (with cross sections of
very different size)

staggered joint of different
cross sections with head plate
and ribs (with cross sections
of very different size)

bolted joint, two head plates
are needed here

Fig. 85: Joints with head plates

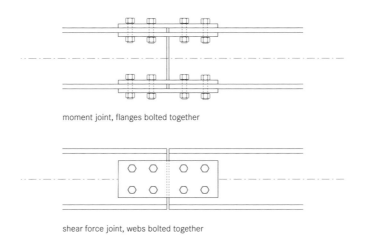

moment joint, flanges bolted together

shear force joint, webs bolted together

Fig. 86: Beam joints

Exactly as with columns, beams can be butt-jointed and welded, Beam joints ensuring a largely undisturbed flow of forces. This can be done in the factory or on the building site. Bolted joints are used exclusively for assembly joints on the building site. Here, strap or head plate joints with high-strength bolts are generally used. Depending on the loads on the building part, the straps must be fixed to the web or the flange, or the connection made by means of a head plate. > Fig. 86

NODES

Nodes always occur at points where several filigree building elements from different planes meet each other. In terms of structural design, node points are always understood as joints, but they cannot always be made as such. They are generally bolted or welded firmly together. There are different ways of making the geometry so that the point of intersection of the element axes is retained. There are ball connections and node plates but also cast nodes, welded nodes or slit nodes. All these connections are used mostly for trusses or space frames. They form the meeting point of slender steel rods. > Fig. 87 There are also points at which cable ends must be connected. Here, too, there are special solutions for securing the cables.

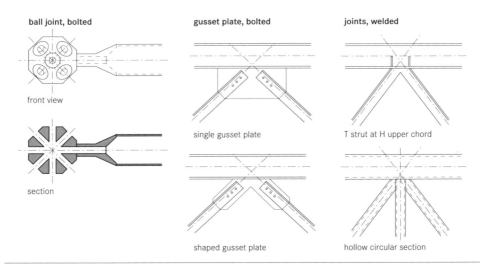

ball joint, bolted

front view

section

gusset plate, bolted

single gusset plate

shaped gusset plate

joints, welded

T strut at H upper chord

hollow circular section

Fig. 87: Examples of node points

ROOF

Steel and other metals can be used in different ways for almost all roof pitches, as roof covering or a roof seal. Roof covering here refers to constructions such as shingles or scales that consist of individual parts and lead water off. The construction is rainproof but not watertight. The more open the way in which the individual elements are laid, the greater the roof slope must be. Metal roof claddings are generally connected on the long side by seams. The transverse joints are made by overlapping, transverse seams or stepped falls. The roofing follows the principle of shingles, although formed shingles are used.

By contrast, a roof seal is watertight. In theory a large watertight layer can be welded out of steel. However, the temperature expansion would be excessive and consequently smaller pieces are used with edge pieces and sealing tapes.

Shaped metal panels can be made from galvanised, rustproof or duplex coated steel. They can be trapezoidal, corrugated, with bar profiles, or in the form of steel shingles. Composite or sandwich panels with thermal insulation can be easily laid as bands.

Steel and metal coverings are very durable and are also suitable for curved surfaces. The pattern of joints helps determine the appearance of the building and should therefore be carefully planned. Since the surface is watertight it is often recommended to lay a double layer with a back ventilation level.

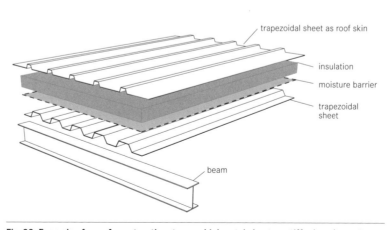

trapezoidal sheet as roof skin

insulation

moisture barrier

trapezoidal sheet

beam

Fig. 88: Example of a roof construction, trapezoidal metal sheet as stiffening element

COMPOSITE CONSTRUCTIONS

The combination of the materials steel and concrete has proved its worth in various forms. In addition to reinforced concrete building parts with steel reinforcement, combining steel sections and reinforced concrete also offers great potential, as it can combine the qualities of both materials. Particularly with regard to fire protection, these building elements can make great sense. In addition, they can give lightweight constructions mass and speed up work on the building site.

In making floor slabs a combination of concrete and steel beams can Composite floor slabs be used as the composite primary construction, or metal sheets can be used together with concrete as a secondary construction. > Fig. 89 Where steel beams form the primary construction they provide a linear support system for in-fill concrete elements and lie within the ceiling plane. The flanges are visible below the ceiling and direct the forces into the columns. Soffits without downstand beams are made; nevertheless, large spans can be covered. Composite floor slabs must be connected with the beams below in a shear-resistant way.

Trapezoidal sheet steel with reinforcement laid in the corrugations can be used as a secondary construction. The package is then laid on top of the steel beams. The trapezoidal sheeting represents a lost formwork. Some kinds of trapezoidal steel sheeting can even replace the lower reinforcement. In the event of fire, the concrete protects the reinforcement, while the sheeting can trap the flaking concrete.

Composite floor slabs can be produced in accordance with these basic principles in a variety of ways. Many manufacturers have exploited the advantages of steel composite floors and offer flexible products. Different variations include the following:

— The trapezoidal sheeting can be used just as the formwork and makes a small contribution to fire protection. Then the steel load-bearing structure lies exposed below the sheeting, the slab is reinforced in the normal way and functions like a ribbed concrete slab.
— If the trapezoidal sheeting is friction locked with the concrete, additional fire protection measures must be introduced, as here the metal sheeting makes an active contribution to the structure. Shear forces are transferred from the concrete to the steel by small projections.
— The beams and the slab can also be connected. This connection is made by means of shear studs on the beam flange. Only the layer above the ribs is structurally effective.
— What are called "integrated floor beams" or also "slim floors" represent a special form, integrating the steel structure into the construction. There are no downstand beams, the soffit is even, and the total construction height is greatly reduced. Only the lower chord of the steel beam is affected in the event of fire. The

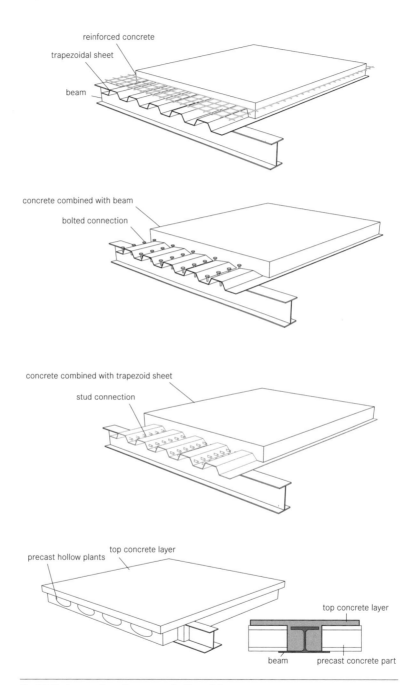

Fig. 89: Various systems for composite floor slabs

connection is more stable than for standard composite floor slabs. Instead of in-situ concrete, precast parts can also be laid on the lower flange, which must then be strengthened appropriately. The precast concrete parts can be prestressed or made as a hollow plank slab, which is particularly light.　　　　　　　　　　　　　■

When producing beams in composite systems, the open areas in the beam are often filled with concrete and additional reinforcement is placed in this concrete. In the event of fire it is above all the web together with the reinforcement that is responsible for the loadbearing capacity of the building element. Welded shear connectors ensure the bond between the steel section and reinforced concrete slab. > Figs. 90 and 91

The connections of composite beams to the columns are commonly made using cleat connections. The connection is without bolts and can be fitted quickly, and the beam is held in position by the subsequently concreted slab.

Composite columns generally consist of hollow sections or rolled sections encased in concrete. In the event of fire, a hollow section quickly becomes very hot on the outside and its structural capacity quickly declines. The concrete then provides stability and the steel serves only to protect it from the heat. Column cross sections filled with concrete retain their loadbearing capacity longer than similarly made composite beams. The forces in a column run along the axis of the building part, whereas a beam fails more quickly due to the weakening of the flange and the ensuing bending.

Profiles entirely encased in concrete resist fire for considerably longer, as they are protected by the concrete. However, temperature fluctuations inside the composite column cause great stresses to develop. Almost all profiles can be used for composite columns but they must be relatively solid and have a concrete cover of at least 5 cm. > Fig. 92

Composite beams

Composite columns

■ **Tip:** Composite floor slabs should always be designed in close collaboration with the building services engineers as the span direction of the beams, design of bearings, distances between beams and openings in the webs for service runs can also have affect the floor slab design. The general services, for example, or a hybrid system for effective room cooling or heating can be easily integrated into the intermediate spaces.

Fig. 90: Effective structural height of the composite beam

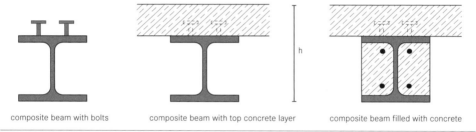

composite beam with bolts | composite beam with top concrete layer | composite beam filled with concrete

Fig. 91: Steel beam with bolts to secure the slab

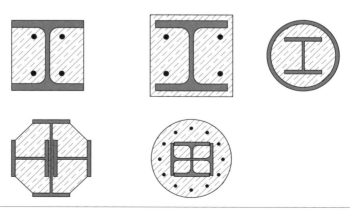

Fig. 92: Examples of cross sections of composite columns

FACADE

In addition to numerous functions as the main loadbearing system for buildings, steel is also very suitable as a loadbearing structure for the building envelope. This means elements that support glass facades, for which steel is almost the ideal material. A variety of systems can be used (see Andreas Achilles and Diane Navratil, *Basics Glass Construction,* Birkhäuser Verlag, Basel 2008).

The post and beam system is the most commonly used construction for glass facades. In this case the post carries the dead weight of the facade and the horizontal wind loads, i.e. it functions as a vertical bending beam. The cross-beams take up part of the wind loads but primarily carry the dead weight of the glass. The beam can run between the posts or, like a continuous beam, can run past them. The beam is generally on a somewhat smaller scale so that the vertical elements are dominant. The grid of the facade and the size of the glass elements have a major impact on the design of the building as a whole.

Post and beam construction

The system of element or panel facades functions very differently. It is made up of individual, prefabricated framed elements including glazing, which then are fixed against the ends of the floor slabs. Regular articulation and elevations with double profiles are characteristic of an element facade. > Fig. 93 They have a high level of prefabrication and can be fitted quickly.

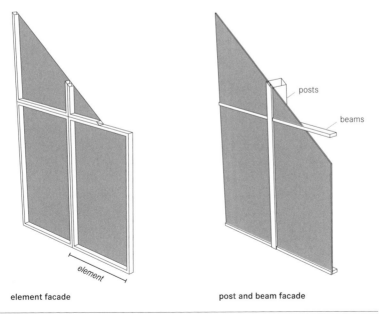

element facade   post and beam facade

Fig. 93: Examples of facade constructions

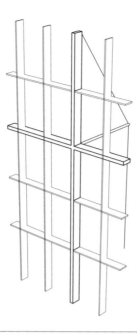

Fig. 94: Articulation of a post and beam facade with secondary structure and trussed posts

A further facade principle is the separation of the facade plane from the loadbearing structural system. Here, an independent steel structure is designed that holds the glazing at a distance. The glass elements are generally fixed by point fixings that are attached to the structural nodes. Above all in point-held facades, but also in combinations with other systems, an independent primary structure for the facade must be made. This can be provided by, for example, lattice girders in a vertical or horizontal direction. Trussed girders can be swivelled around their own axis so that they run vertically in the facade plane. Such girders are often used as a design element with the facade forming the upper chord of the girder.
> Fig. 94

A combination of different systems but also different kinds of glazing, such as structural glazing, is conceivable in many forms. Under some circumstances very complex and highly technical hybrid systems can be developed.

THERMAL SEPARATION

Due to the flexible layering possibilities in steel construction, the danger of thermal bridges forming is very high. Various producers therefore offer elements for the thermal separation of steel building parts. Just

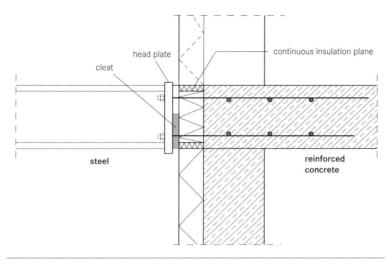

Fig. 95: Thermal separation of steel from a concrete building

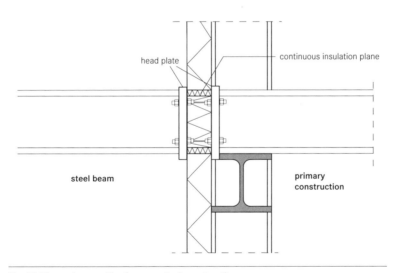

Fig. 96: Thermal separation for pure steel constructions

as in solid construction methods, the separated modules allow freedom in designing cantilevers that penetrate the facade or structural systems outside the building. There are also several options for the connection between concrete building and cantilevered steel elements. > Figs. 95 and 96

In conclusion

The building material steel offers an immense variety of possibilities for construction. Steel buildings provide extremely flexible detailing solutions that can enrich architectural design during the creative process. Hybrid constructions involving other materials or the building services open up new perspectives in design.

Compared to solid building parts and materials, steel structures can be broken up to achieve a maximum filigree quality. Membrane-like cable structures and nets can be just as efficient as large-sized beams. The precise execution that results from a high level of prefabrication provides the designer with a wide range of design options. Constant new developments in material qualities and properties offer exciting prospects for the future.

Alongside the infinite number of technical areas where steel can be used, architecture remains a central focus. In their buildings, architects such as Mies van der Rohe and Jean Prouvé demonstrate a highly skilled combination of structural awareness and design talent. They manage to combine these in a formal idiom that is specific to the material. Precisely this combination of knowledge and creativity must be trained, as it is essentially what constitutes steel construction.

TABLES

Tab. 8: Various kinds of steel profiles

Name	Form	Use	Minimum dimensions (b × h)	Maximum dimensions (b × h)
Wide-flange beams HEA light series HEB normal series HEM strengthened series	HEA HEB HEM	For high loads. Primarily for columns, but also for beams. Also suitable for inclined loading. Special aspect. Only in the HEB series does the profile name match the actual profile height.	HEA 100 (96 mm × 100 mm) 16.7 kg/m HEB 100 (100 mm × 100 mm) 20.4 kg/m HEM 100 (120 mm × 106 mm) 41.8 kg/m	HEA 1000 (990 mm × 300 mm) 272.0 kg/m HEB 1000 (1000 mm × 300 mm) 314.0 kg/m HEM 1000 (1008 mm × 302 mm) 349.0 kg/m
Normal profiles IPN UPN	IPN UPN	More economical than profiles with parallel flanges, the inner angles make them better suited for welded connection. Placing bolts is difficult.	IPN 80 (80 mm × 42 mm) 5.9 kg/m UPN 65 (65 mm × 42 mm) 7.1 kg/m	IPN 600 (600 mm × 215 mm) 199.0 kg/m UPN 400 (400 mm × 110 mm) 71.8 kg/m
Profiles with parallel flanges IPE IPET UPE	IPE IPET UPE	IPE: slender profile, above all suitable as bending beam. UPE: often used in pairs to avoid asymmetrical cross section.	IPE 80 (80 mm × 46 mm) 6.0 kg/m IPET 80 (40 mm × 46 mm) 3.0 kg/m UPE 80 (80 mm × 50 mm) 7.9 kg/m	IPE 600 (600 mm × 220 mm) 122.0 kg/m IPET 600 (300 mm × 220 mm) 61.2 kg/m UPE 400 (400 mm × 115 mm) 72.2 kg/m
Hollow sections RRW/RRK square RRW/RRK rectangular ROR round	square rectangular round	Used almost exclusively for columns and trusses, very good for central loading. RRW = warm made, buckling resistant through compacted corner areas. RRK = cold processed. Light and economical	RRW 40 × 40 (40 mm × 40 mm) 3.4 kg/m RRW 50 × 30 (50 mm × 30 mm) 3.6 kg/m ROR 21.3 (Ø 21.3 mm) 0.9 kg/m	RRW 400 × 400 (400 mm × 400 mm) 191.0 kg/m RRW 400 × 200 (400 mm × 200 mm) 141.0 kg/m ROR 813 (Ø 813 mm) 159.0 kg/m
Round and square steel RND VKT	RND VKT	Mainly for hanging and tension rods. The larger cross sections can also take compression forces (e.g. in concrete composite columns)	RND 10 (Ø 10 mm) 0.6 kg/m VKT 10 (6 mm × 6 mm) 0.3 kg/m	RND 500 (Ø 500 mm) 1540.0 kg/m VKT 200 (200 mm × 200 mm) 314.0 kg/m

Tab. 9: Dimensions of standard IPE profiles

IPE profiles

Abbreviation	Dimensions for						
IPE	h	b	s	t	r	A	G
	mm	mm	mm	mm	mm	cm²	kg/m
80	80	46	3.8	5.2	5	7.6	6.0
100	100	55	4.1	5.7	7	10.3	8.1
120	120	64	4.4	6.3	7	13.2	10.4
140	140	73	4.7	6.9	7	16.4	12.9
160	160	82	5.0	7.4	9	20.1	15.8
180	180	91	5.3	8	9	23.9	18.8
200	200	100	5.6	8.5	12	28.5	22.4
220	220	110	5.9	9.2	12	33.4	26.2
240	240	120	6.2	9.8	15	39.1	30.7
270	270	135	6.6	10.2	15	45.9	36.1
300	300	150	7.1	10.7	15	53.8	42.2
330	330	160	7.5	11.5	18	62.6	49.1
360	360	170	8	12.7	18	72.2	57.1
400	400	180	8.6	13.5	21	84.5	66.3
450	450	190	9.4	14.6	21	98.8	77.6
500	500	200	10.2	16	21	116	90.7
550	550	210	11.1	17.2	24	134	106
600	600	220	12	19	24	156	122

Tab. 10: Dimensions of standard HE-A profiles

HE-A profiles

Abbreviation	Dimensions for						
HE-A	h	b	s	t	r	A	G
	mm	mm	mm	mm	mm	cm²	kg/m
100	96	100	5	8	12	21.2	16.7
120	114	120	5	8	12	25.3	19.9
140	133	140	5.5	8.5	12	31.4	24.7
160	152	160	6	9	15	38.8	30.4
180	171	180	6	9.5	15	45.5	35.5
200	190	200	6.5	10	18	54.8	42.3
220	210	220	7	11	18	64.3	50.5
240	230	240	7.5	12	21	76.8	60.3
260	250	260	7.5	12.5	24	86.8	68.2
280	270	280	8	13	24	97.3	76.4
300	290	300	8.5	14	27	112	88.3
320	310	300	9	15.5	27	124	97.6
340	330	300	9.5	16.5	27	133	105
360	350	300	10	17.5	27	143	112
400	390	300	11	19	27	159	125
450	440	300	11.5	21	27	178	140
500	490	300	12	23	27	198	155
550	540	300	12.5	24	27	212	166
600	590	300	13	25	27	226	178
650	640	300	13.5	26	27	242	190
700	690	300	14.5	27	27	260	204
800	790	300	15	28	30	286	224
900	890	300	16	30	30	320	252
1000	990	300	16.5	31	30	347	272

Tab. 11: Dimensions of standard HE-B profiles

HE-B profiles

Abbreviation	Dimensions for						
HE-B	h	b	s	t	r	A	G
	mm	mm	mm	mm	mm	cm²	kg/m
100	100	100	6	10	12	26.0	20.4
120	120	120	6.5	11	12	34.0	26.7
140	140	140	7	12	12	43.0	33.7
160	160	160	8	13	15	54.3	42.6
180	180	180	8.5	14	15	65.3	51.2
200	200	200	9	15	18	78.1	61.3
220	220	220	9.5	16	18	91.0	71.5
240	240	240	10	17	21	106	83.2
260	260	260	10	17.5	24	118	93.0
280	280	280	10.5	18	24	131	103
300	300	300	11	19	27	149	117
320	320	300	11.5	20.5	27	161	127
340	340	300	12	21.5	27	171	134
360	360	300	12.5	22.5	27	181	142
400	400	300	13.5	24	27	198	155
450	450	300	14	26	27	218	171
500	500	300	14.5	28	27	239	187
550	550	300	15	29	27	254	199
600	600	300	15.5	30	27	270	212
650	650	300	16	31	27	286	225
700	700	300	17	32	27	306	241
800	800	300	17.5	33	30	334	262
900	900	300	18.5	35	30	371	291
1000	1000	300	19	36	30	400	314

Tab. 12: Dimensions of standard HE-M profiles

HE-M profiles

Abbreviation	Dimensions for						
HE-M	h	b	s	t	r	A	G
	mm	mm	mm	mm	mm	cm²	kg/m
100	120	106	12	20	12	53.2	41.8
120	140	126	12.5	21	12	66.4	52.1
140	160	146	13	22	12	80.6	63.2
160	180	166	14	23	15	97.1	76.2
180	200	186	14.5	24	15	113	88.9
200	220	206	15	25	18	131	103
220	240	226	15.5	26	18	149	117
240	270	248	18	32	21	200	157
260	290	268	18	32.5	24	220	172
280	310	288	18.5	33	24	240	189
300	340	31	21	39	27	303	238
320/305	320	304	16	29	27	225	177
320	359	309	21	40	27	312	245
340	377	309	21	40	27	316	248
360	395	308	21	40	27	319	250
400	432	307	21	40	27	326	256
450	378	307	21	40	27	335	263
500	524	306	21	40	27	344	270
550	572	306	21	40	27	354	278
600	620	305	21	40	27	364	285
650	668	305	21	40	27	374	293
700	716	304	21	40	27	383	301
800	814	303	21	40	30	404	317
900	910	302	21	40	30	424	333
1000	1008	302	21	40	30	444	349

Tab. 13: Dimensions of standard square tubes

Square hollow structural sections

a mm	s mm	A cm²	G kg/m	a mm	s mm	A cm²	G kg/m
70	3	7.8	6.1	180	5	34.1	26.8
	4	10.1	8.0		6.3	42.4	33.3
	5	12.1	9.5		8	52.8	41.5
					10	63.7	50.0
					12.5	77.0	60.5
80	3	9.0	7.1	200	6.3	47.5	37.3
	4	11.8	9.2		8	59.2	46.5
	5	14.1	11.1		10	71.7	56.3
90	3	10.2	8,0	220	6.3	52.5	41.2
	3.2	10.9	8.5		8	65.6	51.5
	4	13.3	10.5		10	79.7	62.6
	5	16.1	12.7				
	6.3	19.7	15.5				
100	3	11.4	9.0	260	8	78.4	61.6
	4	15.0	11.7		10	95.7	75.1
	5	18.1	14.2		12.5	117.0	81.1
	6.3	22.3	17.5				
110	3	12.6	9.9	280	8	84.8	66.6
	4	16.6	13.0		10	104.0	81.4
	5	20.1	15.8		12.5	127.0	99.7
	6	23.7	18.6				
120	4	18.2	14.3	300	8	91.2	71.6
	5	22.1	17.4		10	112.0	87.7
	6.3	27.3	21.4		12.5	137.0	108.0
	7	30.0	23.5				
	8	33.6	26.4				
125	4	18.9	14.9	320	8	97.6	76.6
	5	23.1	18.2		10	120.0	94.0
	6	27.3	21.4		12.5	147.0	115.0
					16	188.0	148
140	4	21.3	16.8	360	10	137.0	108.0
	5	26.1	20.5		12.5	170.0	133.0
	6.3	32.3	25.4		161	214.0	168.0
	7	35.5	27.9				
				400	12.5	190.0	149.0
					20	294.0	231.0

Tab. 14: Dimensions of standard rectangular tubes

Rectangular hollow sections

h×b in mm	s mm	r mm	A cm²	G kg/m
100×40	3	6	7.8	6.12
	4	8	10.1	7.96
100×50	4	8	10.9	8.59
	5	12.5	13.1	10.3
100×60	4	8	11.8	9.22
	5	12.5	14.1	11.1
120×60	4	8	13.4	10.5
	5	12.5	16.1	12.7
	6.3	15.8	19.7	15.5
120×80	5	12.5	18.1	14.2
	6.3	15.8	22.3	17.5
120×100	6	15	23.7	18.6
	7	17.5	27.2	21.3
140×70	5	12.5	19.1	15
140×80	4	8	16.6	13
	5	12.5	20.1	15.8
	6.3	15.8	24.8	19.4
	7	17.5	27.2	21.3
150×50	4	8	14.9	11.7
	5	12.5	18.1	14.2
	6	15	21.3	16.7
150×100	6.3	15.8	28.6	22.4
160×80	4	8	18.2	14.3
	5	12.5	22.1	17.4
160×90	5	12.5	23.1	18.2
	8	20	35.2	27.6
180×80	5	12.5	24.1	18.9
	6	15.0	28.5	22.4
	8	20	36.8	28.9
180×100	4	8	21.4	16.8
	5	12.5	26.1	20.5
	6.3	15.8	32.3	25.4
200×120	6.3	15.8	37.4	29.3
	10	30	55.7	43.7
220×120	6	15.0	38.1	29.9
	8.8	26.4	53.4	41.9
320×180	8.8	17.6	82.9	65.1
	12.5	25	115	90.0
400×260	11	22.0	137	108
	17.5	35	211	166

Tab. 15: Dimensions of standard profiles for round-edged U profiles

U profiles (channels)

Abbreviation	Dimensions for						
U	h	b	s	t	r	A	G
	mm	mm	mm	mm	mm	cm²	kg/m
30×15	30	15	4	4.5	2	2.21	1.74
30	30	33	5	7	3.5	5.44	4.26
40×20	40	20	5	5	2.5	3.66	2.87
40	40	35	5	7	3.5	6.21	4.87
50×25	50	25	5	6	3	4.92	3.86
50	50	38	5	7	3.5	7.12	5.59
60	60	30	6	6	3	6.46	5.07
65	65	42	5.5	7.5	4	9.03	7.09
80	80	45	6	8	4	11.0	8.64
100	100	50	6	8.5	4.5	13.5	10.6
120	120	55	7	9	4.5	17.0	13.4
140	140	60	7	10	5	20.4	16.0
160	160	65	7.5	10.5	5.5	24.0	18.8
180	180	70	8	11	6.5	28.0	22.0
200	200	75	8.5	11.5	6	32.2	25.3
220	220	80	9	12.5	6.5	37.4	29.4
240	240	85	9.5	13	6.5	42.2	33.2
260	260	90	10	14	7	48.3	37.9
280	280	95	10	15	7.5	53.3	41.8
300	300	100	10	16	8	58.8	46.1
320	320	100	14	17.5	8.75	75.8	59.5
350	350	100	14	16	8	77.3	60.6
380	380	102	13.5	16	8	80.4	63.1
400	400	110	14	18	9	91.5	71.8

Tab. 16: Dimensions of standard round steel pipes

Round steel pipes

External diameter		Dimensions			
D mm	D inches	s mm	d mm	A cm²	G kg/m
20		2	16	1.13	0.89
21.3		2	17.3	1.21	0.96
25		2	21	1.45	1.13
30		2.6	24.8	2.24	1.76
33.7		2.6	28.5	2.54	1.99
38		2.6	32.8	2.89	2.29
42.4		2.6	37.2	3.25	2.57
44.5		2.6	39.3	3.42	2.70
48.3		2.6	43.1	3.73	2.95
51	2	2.6	45.8	3.95	3.12
54	2 1/8	2.6	48.8	4.20	3.30
57	2 1/4	2.9	51.2	7.93	3.90
60.3	2 3/4	2.3	55.7	4.19	3.31
		2.9	54.4	5.23	4.14
63.5	2 1/2	2.9	57.7	5.52	4.36
70.0	2 3/4	2.6	64.8	5.51	4.35
		2.9	64.2	6.11	4.85
73	3	2.9	67.2	6.39	5.01
76.1	3	2.9	70.3	6.57	5.28
82.5	3 1/4	2.6	77.3	6.53	5.16
		3.2	76.1	7.97	6.31
88.9	3 1/2	3.2	82.5	8.62	6.81
101.6	4	2.9	95.8	8.99	7.11
		3.6	94.4	11.1	8.76
108	4 1/4	3.6	101.8	11.8	9.33
114.3	4 1/2	3.6	107.1	12.5	9.90
127	5	4	119	15.5	12.2
133	5 1/4	4	125	16.2	12.8
139.7	5 1/2	4	131.7	17.1	13.5
152.4	6	4	144.4	18.6	14.7
	6	4.5	143.4	20.9	16.4
159	6 1/4	4.5	150	21.6	17.1
168.3	6 5/8	4.5	159.3	23.2	18.1
177.8	7	5	167.8	27.1	21.3
193.7	7 5/8	4.5	184.7	26.7	21.0
		5.6		33.1	26.0
219.1	8 5/8	6.3	206.5	42.1	33.1
244.5	9 5/8	6.3	241.9	47.1	37.1
267	10 1/2	6.3	254.4	51.6	40.6
273	10 3/4	6.3	260.4	52.8	41.6
298.5	11 3/4	5.6		51.5	40.5
		7.1	284.3	65.0	51.1
323.9	12 3/4	7.1	309.7	70.7	55.6
355.6	14	5.6	344.4	61.6	48.2
		8	339.6	87.4	68.3
406.4	16	6.3	393.8	79.2	62.4

Tab. 17: Dimensions of standard profiles for trapezoidal profiles

Trapezoidal description	Profile cross section	Nominal sheet thickness	Dead weight	Span limits	
		t_N	g	l_{gr1}	l_{gr2}
	Dimensions in mm	mm	kN/m²	m	m
35/207		0.75	0.073	0.89	1.10
		0.88	0.085	1.36	1.70
		1.00	0.097	1.78	2.22
		1.25	0.121	4.40	5.50
40/183		0.75	0.082	1.20	1.50
		0.88	0.096	2.70	3.38
		1.00	0.109	3.90	4.88
		1.25	0.137	5.10	6.38
48.5/250		0.75	0.075	1.77	2.21
		0.88	0.088	2.50	3.13
		1.00	0.100	2.86	3.57
		1.25	0.125	3.60	4.50
38/280		0.75	0.080	3.50	4.38
		0.88	0.094	4.93	6.16
		1.00	0.107	5.63	7.04
		1.25	0.134	7.10	8.88
98/287		0.75	0.087	4.64	5.80
		0.88	0.102	7.06	8.83
		1.00	0.116	8.07	10.10
		1.25	0.145	10.20	12.70
100/257		0.75	0.090	4.70	5.87
		0.88	0.106	5.79	7.24
		1.00	0.120	6.80	8.50
		1.25	0.150	8.57	10.71
126/326		0.75	0.092	4.87	6.09
		0.88	0.108	6.85	8.56
		1.00	0.123	7.30	9.13
		1.25	0.153	8.65	10.70
135/310		0.75	0.097	5.80	7.25
		0.88	0.114	7.80	9.75
		1.00	0.129	8.51	10.64
		1.25	0.161	9.83	12.29
153/280		0.75	0.107	7.75	9.69
		0.88	0.126	10.00	12.50
		1.00	0.143	11.40	14.30
		1.25	0.179	14.40	18.00
165/250		0.75	0.120	8.25	10.31
		0.88	0.141	9.68	12.10
		1.00	0.160	11.00	13.75
		1.25	0.200	13.75	15.00

STANDARDS AND GUIDELINES

DIN EN 502, Roofing products from metal sheet – Specification for fully supported roofing products of stainless steel sheet

DIN EN 508, Roofing and cladding products from metal sheet – Specification for self-supporting of steel, aluminium or stainless steel sheet

DIN EN 1011, Welding – Recommendations for welding of metallic materials

DIN EN 1043, Destructive test on welds in metallic materials – Hardness testing – Part 1: Hardness test on arc welded joints; Part 2: Microhardness testing of welded joints

DIN EN 1090, Execution of steel structures and aluminium structures

DIN EN 1065, Adjustable telescopic steel props – Product specifications, design and assessment by calculation and tests

DIN EN 1991, Eurocode 1: Actions on structures

DIN EN 1993, Eurocode 3: Design of steel structures

DIN EN 1994, Eurocode 4: Design of composite steel and concrete structures

DIN EN 1998, Eurocode 8: Design of structures for earthquake resistance

DIN EN 10020, Definition and classification of grades of steel

DIN EN 10021, General technical delivery conditions for steel products

DIN EN 10024, Hot-rolled taper flange I sections – Tolerances on shape and dimensions

DIN EN 10025, Hot rolled products of structural steels

DIN EN 10027, Designation systems for steels

DIN EN 10029, Hot-rolled steel plates 3 mm thick or above – Tolerances on dimensions and shape

DIN EN 10079, Definition of steel products

DIN EN 10083, Steels for quenching and tempering

DIN EN 10088, Stainless steels

DIN EN 10130, Cold rolled low carbon steel flat products for cold forming

DIN EN 10152, Electrolytically zinc coated cold rolled steel flat products for cold forming – Technical delivery conditions

DIN EN 10162, Cold-rolled steel sections – Technical delivery conditions – Dimensional and cross-sectional tolerances

DIN EN 10163, Delivery requirements for surface condition of hot-rolled steel plates, wide flats and sections

DIN EN 10204, Metallic products – Types of inspection documents

DIN EN 10210, Hot finished structural hollow sections of non-alloy and fine grain steels

DIN EN 10219, Cold formed welded structural hollow sections of non-alloy and fine grain steels

DIN EN 10250, Open die steel forgings for general engineering purposes

DIN EN 10277, Bright steel products – Technical delivery conditions

DIN EN 10278, Dimensions and tolerances of bright steel products

DIN EN 10293, Steel castings – Steel castings for general engineering uses

DIN EN 10343, Steels for quenching and tempering for construction purposes Technical delivery conditions

DIN EN 10346, Continuously hot-dip coated steel flat products - Technical delivery conditions

DIN EN 13381, Test methods for determining the contribution to the fire resistance of structural members

DIN EN 13501, Fire classification of construction products and building elements

DIN EN 14509, Self-supporting double skin metal faced insulating panels - Factory made products - Specifications

DIN EN 15251, Indoor environmental input parameters for design and assessment of energy
performance of buildings addressing indoor air quality, thermal environment, lighting and
acoustics

DIN EN 15804, Sustainability of construction works – Environmental product declarations –
Core rules for the product category of construction products

DIN EN ISO 148, Metallic materials - Charpy pendulum impact test

DIN EN ISO 2063, Thermal spraying - Metallic and other inorganic coatings - Zinc, aluminium and
their alloys

DIN EN ISO 5173, Destructive tests on welds in metallic materials - Bend tests

DIN EN ISO 6508, Metallic materials – Rockwell hardness test

DIN EN ISO 6506, Metallic materials – Brinell hardness test

DIN EN ISO 6507, Metallic materials – Vickers hardness test

DIN EN ISO 6892, Metallic materials – Tensile test

DIN EN ISO 6946, Building components and building elements – Thermal resistance and thermal
transmittance – Calculation method

DIN EN ISO 8990, Thermal insulation – Determination of steady-state thermal transmission
properties – Calibrated and guarded hot box

DIN EN ISO 10113, Metallic materials – Sheet and strip

DIN EN ISO 12 944, Paints and varnishes - Corrosion protection of steel structures by protective
paint systems

DIN EN ISO 14713, Zinc coatings – Guidelines and recommendations for the protection against
corrosion of iron and steel in structures – Part 1: General principles of design and corrosion
resistance

DIN EN ISO 16276, Corrosion protection of steel structures by protective paint systems –
Assessment of, and acceptance criteria for, the adhesion/cohesion (fracture strength)
of a coating

ISO 21930, Sustainability in building construction – Environmental declaration of building
products

ISO 21931, Sustainability in building construction – Framework for methods of assessment of
the environmental performance of construction works

ISO 15686, Buildings and constructed assets – Service life planning

Euronorm 19:57, IPE joists with parallel flanges. Dimensions

Euronorm 24:62, Narrow flange I-beams, steel channels. Permissible deviations

Euronorm 44:63, Hot-rolled IPE joists. Rolling tolerances

Euronorm 53:62, Broad flanged beams with parallel sides. Dimensions

Euronorm 54:80, Small hot-rolled steel channels

Euronorm 55:80, Hot-rolled equal flange Ts with radiused root and toes in steel

Euronorm 56:77, Hot-rolled equal angles (with radiused root and toes)

Euronorm 57:78, Hot-rolled unequal angles (with radiused root and toes)

Euronorm 58:78, Hot-rolled flats for general purposes

Euronorm 59:78, Hot-rolled square bars for general purposes

Euronorm 60:77, Hot-rolled round bars for general purposes

LITERATURE

William Addis: *The Art of the Structural Engineer,* Artemis, London 1994

Edward Allen: *Fundamentals of Building Construction: Materials and Methods,* 6th ed., Hoboken, Wiley, New Jersey 2014

Alan Blanc, Michael McEvoy and Roger Plank: *Architecture and Construction in Steel,* E & F N Spon, London, New York 1993

Terri Meyer Boake: *Understanding Steel Design – An Architectural Design Manual,* Birkhäuser, Basel 2012

Terri Meyer Boake: *Diagrid Structures. Systems, Connections, Details,* Birkhäuser, Basel 2014

Andrea Deplazes (ed.): *Constructing Architecture,* Birkhäuser, Basel 2013

Manfred Hegger: *Basics Materials,* Birkhäuser, Basel 2007

Ulf Hestermann and Ludwig Rongen: *Frick/Knöll Baukonstruktionslehre 1,* Springer Fachmedien Wiesbaden GmbH, Wiesbaden 2015

Ulf Hestermann and Ludwig Rongen: *Frick/Knöll Baukonstruktionslehre 2,* Springer Vieweg, Wiesbaden 2013

Institut für Internationale Architektur Dokumentation: *Featuring Steel Resources, Architecture, Reflections,* Detail, Munich 2009

Ulrich Knaack (et al.): *Facades. Principles of Construction,* 2nd ed., Birkhäuser, Basel 2014

Ulrich Knaack (et al.): *Prefabricated Systems, Principles of Construction,* Birkhäuser, Basel 2012

Ulrich Knaack (et al.): *Components and Connections, Principles of Construction,* Birkhäuser, Basel 2012

Alfred Meistermann: *Basics Loadbearing Systems,* Birkhäuser, Basel 2007

Mario George Salvadori: *The Art of Construction: Projects and Principles for Beginning Engineers and Architects,* 3rd ed., Chicago Review Press, Chicago 1990

Helmut C. Schulitz: *Steel Construction Manual,* Birkhäuser, Basel, Boston 2000

PICTURE CREDITS

Wikimedia Commons - http://commons.wikimedia.org/wiki/File:Olympiapark_und_Olympiastadion_in_M%C3%BCnchen._04_orig.jpg#/media/File:Olympiapark_und_Olympiastadion_in_M%C3%BCnchen._04_orig.jpg

Figures 10, 14, 21, 36, 52, 69, 72, 81, 82, 90: Prof. Dr.-Ing. Bert Bielefeld

THE AUTHOR

Katrin Hanses, M.A., architect, is a research associate in the department of building construction and design at Siegen University and runs her own architecture practice in Cologne.

ALSO AVAILABLE FROM BIRKHÄUSER:

Design
Basics Design and Living
Jan Krebs
ISBN 978-3-7643-7647-5

Basics Design Ideas
Bert Bielefeld,
Sebastian El khouli
ISBN 978-3-7643-8112-7

Basics Design Methods
Kari Jormakka
ISBN 978-3-03821-520-2

Basics Materials
M. Hegger, H. Drexler, M. Zeumer
ISBN 978-3-7643-7685-7

Basics Spatial Design
Ulrich Exner, Dietrich Pressel
ISBN 978-3-7643-8848-5

Basics Barrier-Free Planning
Isabella Skiba, Rahel Züger
ISBN 978-3-7643-8959-8

Available as a compendium:
Basics Architectural Design
Bert Bielefeld (ed.)
ISBN 978-3-03821-560-8

Fundamentals of Presentation
Basics Freehand Drawing
Florian Afflerbach
ISBN 978-3-03821-545-5

Basics Architectural Photography
Michael Heinrich
ISBN 978-3-7643-8666-5

Basics CAD
Jan Krebs
ISBN 978-3-7643-8109-7

Basics Modelbuilding
Alexander Schilling
ISBN 978-3-0346-1331-6

Basics Technical Drawing
Bert Bielefeld, Isabella Skiba
ISBN 978-3-0346-1326-2

Available as a compendium:
Basics Architectural Presentation
Bert Bielefeld (ed.)
ISBN 978-3-03821-527-1

Construction
Basics Concrete Construction
Katrin Hanses
ISBN 978-3-0356-0362-0

Basics Facade Apertures
Roland Krippner,
Florian Musso
ISBN 978-3-7643-8466-1

Basics Glass Construction
Andreas Achilles,
Diane Navratil
ISBN 978-3-7643-8851-5

Basics Loadbearing Systems
Alfred Meistermann
ISBN 978-3-7643-8107-3

Basics Masonry Construction
Nils Kummer
ISBN 978-3-7643-7645-1

Basics Roof Construction
Tanja Brotrück
ISBN 978-3-7643-7683-3

Basics Timber Construction
Ludwig Steiger
ISBN 978-3-7643-8102-8

Available as a compendium:
Basics Building Construction
Bert Bielefeld (ed.)
ISBN 978-3-0356-0372-9

Professional Practice
Basics Tendering
Tim Brandt,
Sebastian Franssen
ISBN 978-3-7643-8110-3

Basics Project Planning
Hartmut Klein
ISBN 978-3-7643-8469-2

Basics Site Management
Lars-Phillip Rusch
ISBN 978-3-7643-8104-2

Basics Time Management
Bert Bielefeld
ISBN 978-3-7643-8873-7

Basics Budgeting
Bert Bielefeld, Roland Schneider
ISBN 978-3-03821-532-5

Available as a compendium:
Basics Project Management
Architecture
Bert Bielefeld (ed.)
ISBN 978-3-03821-462-5

Urbanism
Basics Urban Building Blocks
Thorsten Bürklin,
Michael Peterek
ISBN 978-3-7643-8460-9

Basics Urban Analysis
Gerrit Schwalbach
ISBN 978-3-7643-8938-3

**Building Physics/
Building Services**
Basics Room Conditioning
Oliver Klein, Jörg Schlenger
ISBN 978-3-7643-8664-1

Basics Water Cycles
Doris Haas-Arndt
ISBN 978-3-7643-8854-6

Landscape Architecture
Basics Designing with Plants
Regine Ellen Wöhrle,
Hans-Jörg Wöhrle
ISBN 978-3-7643-8659-7

Basics Designing with Water
Axel Lohrer, Cornelia Bott
ISBN 978-3-7643-8662-7

www.birkhauser.com

Series editor: Bert Bielefeld
Concept: Bert Bielefeld, Annette Gref

Translation from German into English:
James Roderick O'Donovan
English copy editing: Monica Buckland
Project management: Petra Schmid
Layout, cover design and typography:
Andreas Hidber
Typesetting and production: Amelie Solbrig

Library of Congress Cataloging-in-Publication
data
A CIP catalog record for this book has been
applied for at the Library of Congress.

Bibliographic information published by the
German National Library
The German National Library lists this publica-
tion in the Deutsche Nationalbibliografie;
detailed bibliographic data are available on the
Internet at http://dnb.dnb.de.

This publication is also available in a German
language edition (ISBN 978-3-0356-0364-4).

© 2015 Birkhäuser Verlag GmbH, Basel
P.O. Box 44, 4009 Basel, Switzerland
Part of Walter de Gruyter GmbH, Berlin/Boston

Printed on acid-free paper produced from
chlorine-free pulp. TCF ∞

Printed in Germany

ISBN 978-3-0356-0370-5

9 8 7 6 5 4 3 2 1

www.birkhauser.com